Int

When I sit and think of all the time that has gone by already and I have not written a word, I think what a waste. The Angels have been after me for years to write. No matter how much they prod me, I sit and wonder what I would even write about. I am an avid Horror novel fan; Vampire books strike my fancy quite a bit. They struck me enough to try to write a horror novel but after writing a couple of chapters, I put the book down and never picked it up again. As much as I love horror, it was not for me. So after that experience I didn't think of writing again except for every time someone has read my cards and told me that is what I should be doing. So after much contemplation, much compliments in my eloquence when writing emails or blogs, I am faced once again with the need to WRITE.

I recently read a wonderful book about a woman's experience in her own historical house. I could not put the book down. It reminded me of my own experiences and how I felt when they happened. Her writing not only inspired me to develop my own gifts in the Metaphysical world but also I felt such a deep profound connection to her and her house. I felt like I could be right there with her. I am not kidding folks! I would seriously hop a plane tomorrow to go stay with her for a week if I could. In the next couple of days I will be going to purchase her second book and am anticipating the same feelings I had with the first.

Ever since I read her book I have not been able to stop thinking of her, her house, connecting with the spirit world, my own paranormal investigations, the gift of sight that has been covered up over time. I have a strong desire to bring it all back. I want to develop my ability to hear the other side and be able to decipher the whisperings to figure out what message they have for me or for others. I want to be able to help them find their place in this world. I want them to know they have choices and if they want to go to where they can be happy. I want to help make that happen for them. Some of course, will choose not to go as they stay attached to people, places, and objects. Some of them just want more life to live so they live vicariously through their loved ones instead. Whatever their reason may be, I am here to find out what they want and try to help them as much as I can. I also want to help those who are frightened by the spirits that refuse to leave. Making them feel comfortable in their own home again and taking back power is a very important thing to me. After all I have experienced, I feel I can help offer solutions that will work for them and their families without them having to move from their homes or feel terrified staying in them.

I feel for the first time in years, it is clear to me what I should be writing about and that is, what I know best…Ghosts!

In this book I hope to share as much of me as I can with the world so that people like the woman whose book I read and others out there that they are not alone. There are in fact, a lot more of us out here than you realize. Most people do not like to speak out because they fear they will be persecuted for what they have experienced so they hide it and keep it to themselves. Some suffer many years in a home and some of them even literally go crazy because they have hid it for so long, they believe themselves to be less than sane.

If you find yourself reading my book you are either curious about the paranormal or you yourself have had experiences and want to connect with someone else. I am that someone and you are holding the right book. Honestly for either reason, I believe you will not be disappointed by what you are about to read. Please keep in mind, these are my personal experiences and are not opinions nor are they scientific fact. They are experiences for my own that I wish to share with you.

Thank you for taking the time to open my book and begin enjoying my journey through a paranormal life.

Chapter I

The Growing Years

I do not remember a huge portion of my childhood and to this day I still cannot figure out why. I am hoping with some work with the Angels and Ascended Masters, I will be able to figure out the missing pieces. I would love to do a historical check on my family but first I need to check myself. Keep in mind I am sharing with you the things I can vividly remember so it can paint a very clear image in your mind.

I grew up in a single parent household. My mother worked very hard and sometimes more than one job at a time to support me. It would have been easier financially for her to give up for adoption but she did not. She fought to keep me by her side. She loved me more than any human being could love one another. She worked so hard to keep food in my mouth and ensure that I had the very best of everything. I remember she bought me a whole entire bedroom set while she still slept on the floor. She always bought me expensive designer clothes for school and bought the very best food you can buy. I can remember her working split-shifts at a restaurant that has now become a HUGE fine dining chain across the U.S. Many politicians and famous folks would eat there on a regular basis. She made excellent tips and had the best reputation in the place. People came in to sit in her section when they ate there. Her beautiful smile and winning personality won them over every time. She knew what she was doing and she reaped its benefits. My mom has always been my personal Hero.

My mom would come home from work every day worn out from lunch rush and still find time to take care of me before she went back to work for the dinner crowd. We lived very well. I always look up to my mother for all the things she has done for me and our family. No one could have cared for me better. To this day it makes me cry to think about back then. My mom and I are very close to say the least. She and I have a special bond that no one can touch. Thanks mom! I love you!

In growing up with my mom working a lot there was not really any time for bias religion. My mom didn't subscribe to any religion in particular. She was like me, a spiritualist even though she did not realize it. She went shopping for quite awhile through different sectors, different types of churches but to this day she still has not found one that subscribes to everything she believes. I believe Unity would be the best but she has not found one around her to try out. Instead she reads a lot of books which is helping her on her spiritual path.

What I do know for sure is that the women on my mother's side of the family were and are "gifted" with various types of abilities. My mother dreams about people who are getting ready to pass over or have within 24 hrs of her having dreamt of them. She has predicted quite a few people's deaths. This definitely is not an ability anyone would actually want but it's there.

Many times mother has "knowing" that something is going to happen. I also possess this ability. She used to call me often for Tarot readings because she was afraid to pick up and deck and try for herself. Recently she called to ask me which is the best deck to start with. My mother finally got a Tarot Deck and is actually going to put her abilities to work! I could not be more thrilled. The way I read Tarot just basically tells you what is already in your own head. They are things that you know already either consciously or subconsciously but the information is always there. It is whether we choose to listen to it or not that is the important key to our growth and development in life.

My grandmother was also "gifted" with sight as was my great grandmother. They have both passed on and I feel that even though I did not know my great grandmother, she comes around me every now and then. I think how she was in life was not who she really was. I think she was perceived as being crazy because she had talents that in that time frame would make you look like you were nuts or a witch. With time gone by, I believe she drove herself nuts with the constant internal conflict. Now maybe I am wrong but that is what I pick up on every time she visits me.

I do not know how far back the history goes on the women in our family and their "gifts" but I do know that there are at least 3 of us. That is enough for me to know that there is something to be said for genetics of the Metaphysical people. It DOES run in the family. If you have a blood relative you may very well have hidden talents you were not aware of. It is always a good thing to look into. If you find yourself interested in things like this then you may have something you did not realize in your bloodline somewhere.

Now since I was not muffled by any one religion, I was free to believe what I really felt in my heart. It took me many years to figure it all out. When you are very young you listen to everything the Angels tell you until you get to an age where everyone tells you what you see and hear is not real, that it is only your imagination. Eventually you believe them because you love and trust them. You want them to be right. You shut out what you hear and see or you reject it. You pass it off as some other explanation. Maybe it was an imaginary friend after all. Far from it!

For years I struggled with what I really believed. Every time I went to a different church with my mother or a friend, I just couldn't stomach the things that these different religions were selling. How could there be so many different versions of a book that is supposed to be of God? Where is the original? Why has it been edited so much? Does anyone really understand what a parable is? These are questions that were *ALWAYS* in the back of mind when I would sit and listen to all the things you should do or you would go to a very dark place and never recover and that God wouldn't forgive you or love you anymore.

I had many questions my friends. There were many unpleasant thoughts by most but very realistic by standards of a Spiritualist in the making. How in the world could a supreme being who supposedly created us out of Love turn and hate us because we aren't living by a set of rules? I could go on but this book isn't about the battle of religion. This is simply so that you can understand me and why I am living the path I am living.

As I mentioned, I do not remember a whole lot about my childhood. One of the first experiences I can remember is living in an apartment in New Orleans East. If you have heard anything about New Orleans is that it is one of the most haunted cities in the U.S. This place makes most cities look mild. So my mom and I were living in an apartment and by that age I was able to be alone while my mom worked. I was young, maybe 8 or 9 years old. I was old enough to fend for myself and keep the door locked, not answer the phone, not go outside, etc. I was in my bedroom and had just gotten done making a homemade Ouija Board. I played with it alone for a little while. This was NOT the first time I had made one and used it totally alone and gotten results. I just cannot recall anything happening after using it until this point. I had the urge to look into the hallway. As I did, I saw a huge black shadow figure standing there. He was so dark and so solid that I could not see the hallway light through him. I was frozen with fear. I was sitting on my bed so I just turned my head away from him in terror. I heard keys in the front door and decided to look back into the hall. When I did, the figure was gone! That was my first TRUE experience with the unknown.

Was it strange that I was making Ouija Boards and using them alone at that age? I'm sure it was. I kept them hidden from my mom and did not tell her I was using it. I thought she would throw them out. She had always been open-minded to tarot readings but did not believe in a grand portion of my experiences throughout my life with the paranormal. She had an experience of her own years later but I will tell you about that in a later chapter.

Again, in New Orleans my mom and I were living in what was known as a "Shot-gun House". It was a duplex basically and instead of it being squared like most homes, it went straight back. You walked in and there was the living room. Next room was the dining room which my mom turned into her bedroom. There was a skinny hallway which was followed by a small bathroom. If you kept walking down the hall then you would get to my room and behind that was the kitchen. It is a strange configuration but very common in New Orleans.

Many nights I can remember being home alone and hearing footsteps on the hardwood floors. I also could not seem to stay in my bedroom for long periods of time. In fact, I often went and crawled into bed with my mother so I could feel safe. She worked a lot so she never noticed the things I was experiencing and at that point I did not tell her anything in fear she would think something was wrong with me. I also hadn't told her about the other apartment before either. I felt she wouldn't believe me or she would tell me it was all in my head. I thought I should just keep my mouth shut and keep it to myself.

We moved around a lot and each time we moved, we moved into places that had a lingering spirit or two. The common denominator of course, was me. I had seen plenty of movies like "Poltergeist" and "The Exorcist" but little did I know that I had any kind of control with things I could see and hear. I also did not try to interact with what I heard and saw until later.

The next place we lived was in a condominium and still in New Orleans. It was a beautiful place. We painted the living room and dining room a really pretty brick red. It had a small kitchen with two bedrooms and two bathrooms. It was the type that had a toilet and sink in each bathroom and then the tub in the middle that connected the two. It was unusual but charming. In the hallway were two pull out doors that revealed the washer and dryer. For a period of time when I was home alone, I would hear things banging against the washer and dryer. I would say out loud "I know you are here, I hear what you are doing". It continued along with almost inaudible giggles and whispers. Soon after my mom found out she was pregnant with my sister. My sister is 16 younger than me. It was her dad that we were with at the time in the condo. He is a non-believer in anything in this realm so we didn't talk to him much about it. My mom had her cards read before she became pregnant. The reader told her that as soon as she relaxed, she would become pregnant. It was what she wanted more than anything in that time frame. She did what she was told and so it happened just as the reader predicted. What was curious is that after she got pregnant, the noises and voices went away. I told my mom that I thought it was my sister checking us out before she decided to make her entry into the world. My mom giggled but did not believe what I said. It was another experience that I put in the back of my mind and went on with my life.

A year or two later we moved to Cincinnati. Nothing unusual happened there. My sister was born and I helped take care of her and my mom. My mom had a c-section so it took her awhile to recover. I was in high school at that point and unfortunately began a lot of heavy drinking. I had already drunk a few times before in New Orleans with a girl my parents saw as a "bad seed". They thought the move would help me get a fresh start. It would have but I made a bad choice time and time again. I was a lost teenager. I had some friends but I never really went out and did anything. I stayed home reading books and listening to music. I had no real drive to get out and "Live".

I was an awkward teen. I never really fit into any of the groups that all high schools have. I had friends out of each but never got into any one in particular. Of course because of my staying home so much, it really made the friends that I did have, stop inviting me to go out and do things. Instead I withdrew and began my downward spiral of drinking.

We were only in Cincinnati for a couple of years and then my mom's husband got a promotion in different city again and so we were off to Sioux City, IA. We moved into a quaint little duplex with an upstairs, mid-level and basement. It was an interesting place but right away I did not like the feel of the basement. I felt uncomfortable to say the least. I did not even like walking by the door leading down to it. Most of the time when my mom and her husband were out, I would make sure that door stayed closed so that when I went to the kitchen I did not have to see the door open and imagine what could be coming up those stairs. Unfortunately the washer and dryer were down there so I had to go face my uncomfortable feelings frequently. Nothing happened to me while I was down there but I definitely had the feeling of not being wanted and that I should do my business and get out. Something was watching me but I did not stick around to find out what.

Our bedrooms were located upstairs. There were three total. At the top of the stairs was a bathroom, then my room, my sister's room and finally my mom's room at the end of the hallway. Often times when home alone I could hear footsteps coming up the stairs and walking down toward my mom's room. It didn't frighten me though so I knew whoever it was wasn't threatening. I kept picking up on a female energy, a young one in her early 20's. I asked her once who she was. I shut my eyes and saw a young bride. Suddenly she changed into a skeleton still in the wedding dress, only torn. I believe she passed on her wedding day tragically. She was looking for someone and she was at ease with us being there. That was my first awareness of an intelligent ghost.

One day I was shut up in my room listening to music like I did very often. My mom was home and was napping in her room. My mom came and opened my door. She said "why did you do that?" She seemed very aggravated with me. I looked at her perplexed and replied "what are you talking about mom?" She said "you woke me up! You were twisting the door knob or something but you woke me up". She was really angry and really believed it was me. My sister slept in a crib and was clearly not her. I told my mom that it was quite impossible since I was in my room the whole time. Annoyed with me, she shut my door.

My mom never really believed that what I said was the truth. I told her about the ghost and that it was probably her. She scoffed and said "I don't think so". Again, I shut my mouth and went about my business. It was strange though, it seemed as though every time I would go to a friend's house to stay over, this ghost would go with me and walk around the house outside as if she were trying to protect me from someone. I was not good at communications at that time so I was not exactly sure why she would do that. It was kind of sweet yet unnerving. I wonder if it was the man that killed her that she was trying to protect me from or perhaps she was lonely and felt she could trust me. Whatever the reason, as long as I lived in that place, she was there.

After a couple of years we moved again. This time it was across the street and a few houses down. It was an actual house instead of a duplex. It was a nice little three bedroom house. It was two stories with a basement. Again, just like the other places, I would hear footsteps all over the house as well as up and down the stairs. I never felt comfortable in my sister's room either. It seemed darker than the other rooms. She often slept with mom and her husband so she didn't spend a lot of time in her room. I think maybe she knew and chose not to sleep in her own room. The rest of the house seemed just fine.

The basement of this house seemed to be calm and so going up and down there was not a problem. The only real problem area I could feel was my sister's room so I stayed out of there unless I had to go in for some reason. It was uncomfortable to even walk by it to go to the bathroom that was in the hallway. Other than the few footsteps every now and then, this house wasn't too bad and we lived there for a couple of years comfortably.

Being a teenager was a rough time and as such, I embraced reading a lot of horror novels and movies. Something about braving things that scare others that gave me such a high. Listening to music got me through a lot of time. I was mostly into punk music and hard rock. Metal soon followed my favorite genres of music. Feeling so connected with another realm also made me drawn to everything else dark. Feeling this way did not help my life as a teenager. It made me feel that much more inadequate and alienated. I thought everyone was convinced I was a total weirdo. I ended up befriending darker type friends. Even in doing that, I still stayed at home a lot.

There was a day where my friends invited me to go out cruising with them. Something was nudging me to stay home. I did just that and it turns out that it was the right thing to do because my friends ended up getting into an accident and one of them ended up dead. I do not know why I felt such a pull to not go but it was there. It wasn't the typical "I just don't feel like it" response. I just literally felt as though it would be a mistake. And a grave mistake it would have been. I think I might have ended up dead myself if I had gone.

Things got really strange for me after all of that. For once the house I lived in was relatively calm but my life was turbulent. I caused my mom and her husband problems once I turned 18. I started drinking again and heavily. I would do stupid things like be gone until late at night then come home at 2a.m. My friends would be so loud and belligerent that it would wake my mom and her husband up. I'm not sure why I was such a mess. I just felt very out of place. I felt as if I was living in the wrong time, wrong century, and wrong life. All I ever really felt was awkward and still sometimes do even now.

After having disturbed the house many times, I was told I needed to move out. I did and moved into my very first apartment. It was on the top floor and had an incredible view. Unfortunately all I did was waste my experience in there by drowning my sorrows and drinking way too much. People were using me and I was o.k. with it. I knew they needed a place to party and I knew I wanted their booze. It worked out great. I had no paranormal experiences to speak of in this apartment. Even if there had been anything in there, I would not have been aware enough to know. I did not care about much of anything in that place. I lost my job because of my inability to get up early on a Sunday morning to go work at a fast food place. I partied every night until I met someone. He made me start to care about life again. He was also drinking but when I got sick, he called my mother. She took me to a doctor to check me out. He put me on medication for my ulcers. I realized that I was not taking good care of myself and so I begged to move back home.

I was allowed back home but under rules of course. I stopped drinking like a fish and started to put myself back together. I was also still soul searching and trying to figure out what my existence was about. Why was I here? Why was I having such strange things happening around me? Why did I feel so alienated and small? Why did I not have a normal life with normal friends? Those questions would be answered in time.

Going back to my origins, I believe I was always meant to help people. I was meant to help the living as well as the dead. Pulling up my beliefs again, ghosts are not all evil and they certainly are not going to "hell". When we were crated we were given free will. So when you really consider it, you understand that even in death we still have free will. Most of those spirits that stick around have done so by choice. They either do not know that they have gone so they keep trying to live what they think it their life. Some of them are caught in a time loop and keep playing out the scene of their death over and over. It is very tragic deaths that cause that type of manifestation. Some ghosts stick around because they feel they were not ready to go. They want to stay to live more life, take care of loved ones, or to take vengeance on the person who caused them harm. And there are some, yes, that were evil people when they were alive and so now in death they hold on because they want to keep hurting people if they can. Fortunately, the vast majority of ghosts I have encountered have been docile with no intent to harm me. They were unguided and not knowing they should or move on or even how to.

Where do I come in? I am here to help the living deal with their loss and to help the dead do the same thing. I am learning to help the dead move on to where they need to be. They always say to tell them to go to the light but in my experience, it sometimes take a lot more than just that. Some of them see the light and just are unwilling to go. Of course there are some that choose to stay no matter what you ask them to do. They want to watch their loved ones, they are attached to their possessions, or attached to a place where they were most happy or most unhappy and are content staying where they are. To those you cannot do anything but let them continue their existence. You can however ask them to stop scaring people. Most of time, it is that easy to accomplish. Only the not so nice ones are hard to convince and sometimes completely inconvincible. It is a battle and not a very nice one I might add.

Up until the last 10 years I had no idea what I was going to be in store for and was not really sure how to react to the things I was experiencing. Even when I started to think of the path I should possibly take, I was not totally on board. I started watching a whole lot of paranormal shows on television and reading as many paranormal stories that I could get my hands on. This continued on and still continues today. My thirst for knowledge and thirst for wanting to know how many others there are out there that are like me is almost overwhelming.

How did I get all the information I have now about Ghosts? It is a combination of personal experiences combined with all the research and study I have done of other people's encounters documented. There are certainly plenty of fictional movies out there that open the door to get people interested but only a few of us actually go out and explore the realm and try to have more experiences to document. Some of the movies put the facts in and some of them are just all a part of the movie glamour.

What information I still do not have is why I have been chosen to do this. Who picked me to do this and for what reason? Do I have something other people do not? Does this make me a freak or does this make me special? I do not know if I will ever have the answer to that question but no matter what happens, I know that my life is very different than most people would dream to be. I realize my life will never be a nice little house in a meadow with a white picket fence. I'll not be the woman with a huge garden and a man that goes out and earns the money to support our dreams. Those things just are not me.

I do have dreams like everyone else. My dreams though, are scary and full of paranormal investigations. My dreams are full of trying to communicate with spirits of another realm. As out there as it is, that is who I am and what I've become.

Can I blame anyone for reading this and saying "geez this girl is really messed up"? Absolutely not! I know I was messed up when I was a kid but after everything I've been through, I am a much stronger person and I know exactly what it is I want out of life. Not everyone can say the same. I just had to go about it in a very different way.

Chapter II

Going through my 20's

After moving out of my parent's home once again, I moved to Omaha, NE with my boyfriend who later became my husband. We moved around a few times ourselves and without paranormal experiences. That changed when we moved into a house apartment. These are interesting places to say the least. They are houses that have been divided up into one bedroom apartments. This place was being run by a company that had several more houses like this one. They didn't do a credit check and the places were furnished. We did not make much money so it made sense to live in a place like this.

We moved in as soon as we could and everything seemed ok for awhile. Then once again as when I was younger, things started to happen. I started to hear footsteps on the stairs in the hall when no one was around, I could hear occasional voices when I knew the neighbors were not home. Things started to escalate after awhile. I can clearly remember being woken up by a loud man's voice. I opened my eyes and could still hear him only the voice was IN the room, not next door. He was speaking either in a different language or speaking backwards. It was very creepy and nothing like I had heard before. I woke up my boyfriend and by the time I did, the voice stopped.

The door that separated the living room from the bedroom was a wooden slat door. It looks like blinds but they are not moveable. Well one night we were in the bedroom with the door shut. Out of nowhere was a very loud bang against that door as if something large and heavy had been thrown against it. We thought maybe someone got into the apartment somehow so we got up and went to look but there was no one there and nothing out of place. The door was still perfectly locked up.

One night we had some friends over. We had all been sitting in the living room when we heard a knock at the door. A guy who we barely knew came over to visit. The guys went into the kitchen and my girlfriends and I stayed in the living room. We decided to pull out one of my homemade Ouija Boards. We were all giggly and asking silly questions when all the sudden the spirit that was coming through was adamant about a particular subject. This spirit spelled out that "they" did not like the guy that was in our kitchen. This was the same guy that had just come over. They continued to spell out they did not like him, he was evil, evil walks with him, and they told us to make him leave. Just after they spelled this out and we were trying to make sense of it, we heard something fall to floor in the kitchen and hear the guys yelp. I got up and ran in there to see what happened. They explained how they were standing there talking and saw a pitcher that was secure on the counter top slide all the way across and then fly off onto the floor. We were all pretty creeped out. I asked to talk to my boyfriend in the other room alone so I could tell him what the spirits had told us about not liking that guy we had over. They also had asked that we never let him in again.

After that experience we indeed did not let that guy come back over to the house. Things calmed down again and all was well. We lived in that apartment for a couple of years and then decided we wanted to move into a different place. Under the same company, we moved into a different apartment about a mile or two down the road. We were closer to things that required walking to since we did not have a car.

Nothing paranormal happened in this place but it is when I started to dabble with Wicca and began reading tarot cards. There was a woman who lived downstairs that was an actual Witch. She did rituals and read tarot cards. She was also a heavy drinker and smoker. She would play her albums sometimes very loudly. On occasion I would go to visit her to let her read my cards. I cannot really remember any of the readings now because they were not very important. Although she had problems, she did help me get more into reading cards. I bought a few different decks and began practicing as often as I could.

Other than being around this woman, doing cards, and working, things stayed relatively calm. A year later that changed. I met more friends that lived in the neighborhood and started to have a life. My boyfriend at the time and I fought a lot so there was always that tension. I dealt with it though and kept going. One of our friends lived right down the street and we use to go hang out with him and his girlfriend at their place. We watched movies and talked a lot. He and his girlfriend also had a nasty history and would have real knock down and "drag em out" fights.

I do remember after knowing them awhile, he showed us their closet in their bedroom. He said he locked the spirits up and banished them to his closet. Walking near it, I felt very uneasy and could tell there was in fact, something in there. You could also clearly see scratch marks on the lower part of the inside of the door. It was very creepy. I do not know what he was into but I suspect he was into dark craft. It scared me but I wasn't sure what to do about it. We left and went home. I did not want to go over there again in fear something would rub off on me.

After that he only came to our place to visit but that too was short lived. It was not too long after that he got into a fairly serious fight with his girlfriend. He decided he would "show" her. He shot himself in the head and died. I would not doubt at all that his spirit is now haunting that apartment. It is sad to think about. This was now my second friend that died.

Time wore on and I got tired of being where I was. I wanted to be near my mother and sister greatly. After arguing about it, I got my boyfriend to move with me to Illinois because that is where they were living at the time.

Once again we moved into a house apartment. This one in particular had four apartments. The downstairs had two and the upstairs had two more. Our landlord actually lived in the apartment right below us as we lived upstairs in the back. We had a nice little sun porch and the place was fully furnished. I had a nice sized kitchen, which is always good for me as I love to cook a lot. The bedroom was also a nice size. The only disconcerting thing was that there was a door from the bedroom that went into the hall we shared with our neighbors. We could have made that our living room but it was cooler to have the living room in the back where all the trees were since we did not have air conditioning. The bedroom would usually cool off by the time night time rolled around so we were good to go with a fan. In the winter it was really cold so we had a nice space heater in there and it worked out.

This was a neat little apartment with a 70's look as far as the furniture was concerned. It was cozy and housed us for a couple of years. As far as paranormal, well, I did have more experiences. I could hear footsteps coming up those back steps when no one was around. We shared that back hallway with our landlord and when friends came to visit they used that hallway as well. The old man worked during the day so when he was not home and neither was anyone else but me, I'd hear someone clearly coming on up the stairs but when I'd go to check it out, no one was there.

One night I woke up to a man standing there with his arms crossed looking at me. It was right in front of the door that separates the bedroom from the hallway. He looked just as solid as any real person and for a split second I thought we had a break-in. This guy was tall, dark shoulder length shaggy hair, black leather jacket and blue jeans on. He looked like a rough biker type of guy. He was just staring at me like he was waiting for me to do something. I was so scared that I tried waking up my boyfriend. By the time I got him up, the biker was gone. It seemed so real and so vivid I didn't know what to think.

I never saw that visitor again thank goodness but I think if I had the chance again I would have asked him who he was and what he wanted. Back then I wasn't sure what to do about this type of stuff though so I just did what I could which was try to gain support of my mate. He didn't see or hear a thing so it didn't help comfort me in any way.

I never heard or saw any of the neighbors socialize so I am not sure if anyone else ever had anything happen in their apartments. So once again I was left thinking that I am the common denominator for all of these spirits. Was I drawing them to me? Did they know I could hear and see them? Did they know before I did that I could actually interact with them?

We only lived in this apartment again for a couple of years, married, and moved back to Nebraska after much dragging of my feet. I did not want to return but I was assured our fights would lessen if we did because he'd be happy again. Boy was I wrong!

So we moved back to Nebraska and back in to yet another house apartment. This was more of a duplex though. Our apartment was upstairs. Nothing really happened there that was paranormal. It was a crappy apartment with crappy neighbors and lots of cockroaches which I despise! The fighting got much worse in this place until I had enough and moved out. That was the end of that.

I met someone else by way of old friends of ours. I was surprised I had never bumped into him before because we had both been friends with these people for years. I think I knew them the longest though because they were also mutual friends of my first husband. Strange I know but we travelled in the same circles almost. The two men did not know each other though.

We quickly got into a relationship and quickly moved in together. We couldn't live with his parents which was where he was living at the time. We ended up moving in to his grandmother's house. She primarily lived downstairs and we stayed upstairs. We had a bathroom of our own and as far as cooking, we had a large microwave. I became quite a cook with a microwave. I can cook just about any of the things I cook in the stove or oven in a microwave as well.

This house was crazy! First what you need to know is that his grandfather died on the porch of this house. This was the last house he had bought that they were repairing and fixing. He died before he could get everything done. So the grandmother was working at a nursing home to pay the bills and was lonely living alone. She was happy to have her grandson there and came to like me living there. She and I became good friends.

In the time we lived there a lot happened! I could be home alone and I'd hear those footsteps downstairs walking around, footsteps coming up the stairs to the top right at the hallway, cigarette smoke as if someone just lit up, and cold breezes on and off when there were no windows open. We had no central air. The only air we had was a huge air conditioner unit in the window but to feel a cold breeze when we didn't have it on and in the middle of the hallway, was very unusual.

While we were there I also became pregnant with our daughter. I was very sick for the first three months and was bedridden for the most part. I didn't pay too much attention to much of what was going on there because my mind was somewhere else. But when I did, I kept hearing voices whispering as if having a conversation that I could just barely hear but could not make out what they were saying. I thought I was going crazy.

After finding out I was pregnant, naturally I wanted my mom. Since her and I were so close, I knew she would help me greatly. We picked up and moved to where my family where which at the time was Pensacola, FL. It was beautiful there. I absolutely loved being back down south. There were lots of palm trees, sand, sun, warmth, and a beach not too far away. It was marvelous.

We moved into the house that my mom and her ex husband had. My sister was a youngster at the time. She was in school so during the day gone as were mom and her husband since they both worked. My guy was also working so I was totally alone during the day.

I began to hear a little girl's voice, giggles, whispers and footsteps on the carpet down the hall. My sister's room always kind of made me feel uneasy so I stayed out of it most of the time unless I had to go in there. When she was in school sometimes I would go sleep in her bed so I could move around freely since I was getting larger and larger.

I clearly remember sleeping in my sister's room one morning. My mom was off work and was in her room sleeping as well. We both had our doors shut. I awoke to hear my mom's voice say something to me. Later I got up, walked out and saw that my mom's door was still shut. She had not been in the room or saying anything to me. I asked her about it when she got up later and she said she definitely did not say anything to me.

My daughter was born in April and I less sleep than before. The experiences seem to taper off. No one was having experiences for the longest time other than me. Later on my mom did hear a little girl's voice when my sister was nowhere around. She did mention it to me but she just blew it off and didn't think about it again. I think she didn't want to believe what she had heard. It was easier to blow it off and remain comfortable in your surroundings.

We moved out into our own apartment and were living a decent life or so I thought but that is another story. During the time we lived in this nice apartment, I became pregnant with our son. I was very sick yet again and so my mother would come get our daughter to care for her while I was bedridden. It was bad enough that if I stood up to go to the restroom, I'd have to run because whatever I ate or drank would come right back out.

Now with one child and another on the way a one bedroom apartment was simply not enough space. We needed to move to a larger place. We started searching around until we found the most beautiful home in the historical district. It was a house that was converted into a duplex. There was an apartment upstairs and another downstairs. We moved into the apartment downstairs. We were so excited. It was so beautiful! It had all wood floors except for the linoleum in the kitchen. The kitchen was large and had an island in the middle with the stove. It was something out of a dream for me. I thought here is my dream home! It ended up being far from that.

We moved in and decided to paint the walls. We picked a lot of contrasting colors that would also blend when doors were open. The front room was a pretty lavender color, the living room was brick red, the kitchen was turquoise and peach, the kid's room was bright yellow, the bathroom was a light blue and we couldn't decide yet on the laundry room. This place was just amazing. There was woodwork everywhere. There were two fireplaces that were just beautiful but they were unusable because they never fixed it to where they could since they made the upstairs into an apartment. So as beautiful as they were we could not use them. There were huge wood sliding doors to separate the front room from the living room. One went into the wall. The bathroom had one of those old antique claw bath tubs. We had a yard all to ourselves because our neighbor was a recluse and didn't use it. We also had use of the driveway as our neighbor always chose to park on the street in front of the house. It was almost as if we had our own house really because we rarely heard our neighbor upstairs. It was just magnificent and inexpensive. The ceilings were high as were the windows. We felt lucky and blessed to have such a place.

After awhile things began to change. The first things to happen were the infestations. Rats were the first of the three infestations. I began noticing that there were holes in the bread bags. I kept them on top of the refrigerator so I found it perplexing that there were holes. I moved the bread into a cabinet after that. One day we were sitting in the living room watching television and a rat just came running out from that door that slides into the wall. He ran right across the room in front of us into the kitchen. We thought how strange that is that he came out in broad daylight in front of us. We didn't know what else to do other than put out poison. We put it behind the sliding door because we figured if there was one there would be more. We could not have pests like this in the house with little ones. The poison worked and we never heard or saw another rat.

The next infestation to occur was wood roaches. These things were massive and typically in a normal circumstance you'd get one or two come in when it rained in particular. In our case they were coming in by handfuls. We sprayed and they died but still they kept coming in. I clearly remember my daughter picking one up and almost putting it in her mouth. She was a toddler and at that age they put everything into their mouths. I was horrified! Eventually though they tapered off and we quit seeing quite so many. We went back to the normal one or two every now and then.

Next up were fleas. Now we did have a cat because we figured if we had one, the roaches and rats would stay away. Cats are excellent hunters after all. Our cat had never been outside. He was strictly an indoor pet. All of the sudden we had a huge infestation of fleas. We do not know if we walked across the yard and picked them up or what happened but there were so many it was unreal. They quickly infested our poor cat to the point where we had to send him out to the vet and get him dipped. We sprayed and sprayed. It was futile; they were not going to leave. They embedded themselves in the wood floors, deep into the cracks. They would wait until the spray dried up and then come right back out.

The time came to when it was time to have my son. I was in the hospital for a week after having had an emergency c-section that went terribly wrong. From what I know I died on the table. They brought me back and gave me a transfusion. I do not have any memories of where I went when it happened but I did know that it did. My ex asked me how I knew that because other than the doctors he was the only one that knew. He hadn't told my mother as to keep her from worrying. It took 6 doctors to save my life.

My doctor sat at my bedside weeping when he was telling me what happened and how they had a hard time putting me back together. It was one of the most miserable times in my life. I was utterly alone at the hospital. My mom was taking care of my daughter and my ex was off supposedly working but again, that is another story. I was alone and couldn't feed my son without the assistance of a nurse because I could barely move. I was very depressed and cried a lot.

While I was out, my ex scrubbed the floors and sprayed again in hopes that when I got home, the fleas would be gone. Unfortunately it didn't work out that way. We arrived home and within the first few hours there was already a flea on our newborn son. I was devastated. Since my state of mind was already skewed due to depression, this broke me down further. I bought a net to put over his sleeper so they couldn't bother him. They kept biting me since I had plenty of blood to go around after the transfusion. Eventually when it got cold outside again, they went away.

Aside from the infestations, there were many other things that occurred in this house. There were many times where I would be home alone because my mother had my daughter and my ex would be off doing his thing. I'd go to take a bath or go to cook some food and I would clearly hear my name called. It always sounded like my ex so I'd turn around thinking he was home. No one was there. I'd also go to take a bath and hear the front door totally unlock, open, close, and lock again. Again, I'd think he was home so I'd say "hey!" and got no response. I'd get out of the tub, dry off and find that there was no one there at all.

When my daughter was gone to my mom's, I always shut her bedroom door because if I didn't, I'd see shadows walking around in her room. This scared me so I closed the door and put a towel under to cover up the crack. Later we discovered that there was a room walled off. It was behind her closet, behind the living room fireplace, and the front entrance hall. If you looked behind that huge sliding door that went into the wall, you could see the room back there. It was very creepy. I kept wondering what happened in that house.

I also notice that my ex and I argued a lot in that house and as soon as we'd leave the house, we were just fine as if nothing was going on. It was the same with our daughter. She would be very cranky and unhappy in the house but when we left, she was happy as can be. The second we drove back up in the driveway she'd get fussy again. When my mother and sister would visit, my mom would get very uncomfortable within a matter of ten to fifteen minutes and she'd have to leave. She'd always say something like "I don't know why but I just don't feel right in here, I have to go". This place really just had a very negative energy. I do not know if there were actual spirits in there or if there was residual energy or beings. Either way this place became very scary to be living in.

One night after our son was born and our daughter was still with my mom, we slept in the living room because it was the warmest room in the house. The baby was bundled and toasty. He was totally knocked out and we were in the process of trying to sleep ourselves. There were no lights in the living room other than the light emanating from the stereo. My ex passed out quickly and I was looking around the room and started to see several shadows dancing around the room. It scared the hell out of me. I didn't know what was going on or why. I also did not know what to do about it so eventually I shut my eyes and forced myself to go to sleep. They obviously were not touching me or doing anything other than walking around so what could I do?

This place that once was the house of my dreams ended up being the house of my nightmares. I have never lived in a scarier place than this. We asked the neighbor upstairs had experienced anything unusual at all and he said he hadn't. He didn't even have any of the infestations we had. It was so strange.

If I could go back and find the new owners of that place, I would love to ask if I could investigate it now. I would love to find out the history behind that house because I'd be willing to bet that something very dark happened there. I wonder even now if the current occupants are experiencing any activity.

In the midst of all the stress this house brought, my relationship was not going much better. He was gone often and my family began to despise him. There was a lot going on. I took friendship with a girl who turned out to be quite an ally later on. She would come over and hang out and offer me her ears as I had no one else to talk to. She also read my palms and gave me quite a reading. She read for not only me but also my ex and mother. She was dead on with what she told us. It was very strange and yet very cool. She didn't seem to pick up on what was going on with the house because she was more in tune with what was going on between him and me. She could not be more right but that would be more confirmed later on. I wish I was in touch with her now. I would love to tell her how right she was and to thank her endlessly for telling me the truth.

The times ahead would only prove to be more stressful and more complex. I know for sure that I was being guided by a force. It was a force I was sure was Angelic. I had gotten a glimpse while I was in the hospital that made me start to consider what I would be in for in the future and just how protected I was. I was as I mentioned, very alone. One day a minister walked in. For once here was someone to see me first and really touch base with me instead of rushing to see the baby and then me as a secondary. As soon as he opened that door, I felt a sheet of calm relief wash over me. I barely knew him. He was a minister at my parent's church at the time. I had met him once. Here he was checking on me. It was so strange to me but the feeling I felt really made me stop for a minute. Years later I figured out the significance.

Chapter III

Growing into the Strange

My ex lost his business and so we couldn't pay the bills and ended up getting evicted. With that, we packed everything we could in the car and headed back to Omaha to where his family was. I did not want to leave but I didn't know what other choice we had at that point. My parents were not in the position to help us out and at this point they did not like my ex so they left it up to me what I was going to do. Our daughter stayed with them and the plan was to get her back after we settled in.

We moved in with his stepfather and sister into their house. After a year of staying there we moved back into his grandmother's house. Again were the familiar experiences happening all over. I heard footsteps, fresh cigarette smoke when no one was home, breezes and voices.

I clearly remember once time I went into the closet to get something. It was dark and I as reaching for the light switch when I felt something touch my rear end. I turned the light on and thought maybe I bumped into something but, there was nothing there that I could have bumped into. I was quite sure that it was his grandfather. I told his grandmother about it and she laughed and said "it sounds like my husband".

The voices I heard became more prevalent and started to get on my nerves. I couldn't make out what they were saying! I said out loud to them once "can you speak up, I can't hear you". Unfortunately it never got loud enough for me to hear. Later I went to a psychic with my ex's mother and grandmother. The woman told me about things so far into my future, I am still living some of it now. She was very accurate. She told me that I would stop hearing the voices and she was right! I asked the Angels actually to remove the voices and after I did, I heard nothing more.

Once again I was in a very stressful situation. My now ex and I had gotten married and decided to make things work despite all the happenings in Florida. We were still not settled enough for our daughter to come back to us and so my parents kept caring for her. I was still very depressed.

One time we all sat up in the bedroom with the Ouija board I had made a year or so before. We talked to the grandfather who told us to get the wiring fixed in the house or there would be a fire. Without delay we had an electrician out who told us the same thing. I wonder what would have happened if we hadn't called. I believe he was telling us the truth. He said things only they would have known so we were positive it was him.

Eventually things happened and my ex's mother needed to move back in so we were to find another place to go because we could not all fit there. Stress became very tight. We did find a place though that he could just barely afford and moved within a couple of months. Unfortunately it was another one bedroom so we still could not bring our daughter home. At this point almost 2 years had elapsed and she was very attached to my parents as they were to her. Next thing I knew they were asking to adopt her because they did not see us getting out of our rut anytime soon. We did agree because we wanted the best for her. To this day I still do not regret the decision. I am also still close to my mom and so I have contact with my daughter as well. She's such a delight and I'm happy to be in her life.

During the time I was living in that house, I started a website dedicated to ghost stories from anyone who would write me with an experience. I would put a main story that was easy to find on the net on the home page. Typically it would be a very well known place. I had two pages that were stocked full with people's experiences as well as my own here and there. I became very good friends with various other sites that dealt with haunted places, ghosts, spirits, horror, and music. I was linked all over the place and had many web awards for my site.

Back then I was known as LadyBarker. That name was derived for my love of my favorite horror novelist. I am sure you can figure out who it is quite easily. Yes aside from my experiences I was very much into horror movies and books. No surprise there really. I was known all over the net by that name but eventually due to lack of finances I had to let my site go. It was very sad and I still miss it to this day. It was the beginning of my path without knowing in which direction it would take.

Now this new apartment brought about more experiences. I should have known right? At first things were calm but over time things started happening. There were noises throughout the apartment that were not coming from the living. You could always hear someone doing something in whatever room you were not in. Upon examining the room, no one was there. This phenomenon was nothing new to me but what was new was the way they went about other things which made me believe this time they were just residual ghosts. During certain hours I could hear things going on the kitchen as if someone was in there cooking and cleaning. I'd go look and of course there was nothing going on and the noise stopped. I think that it was a couple that lived there before that died. They were living out their lives as if they were still alive.

One time my ex walked through the hallway going into the bedroom and I heard him say "excuse me". I went in a few minutes later and asked him who he was talking to and he said "I felt like I bumped into someone in the hall and it was an automatic response to say excuse me". That was yet another confirmation that there was a presence or two there. Often I could feel a presence lingering around in the bedroom. In fact that is where I felt most of my uneasy feelings. It seemed to me that this couple that was living there did not realize we were there and if they did, they thought we were the ghosts. It was much like a movie that was put out a few years back. They do not realize they are dead and so when they encounter us, they think we are intruders or ghosts. It's a very strange phenomena but I think it is also very common.

After a year or two in that apartment we decided to move into a larger apartment across town. This apartment was very nice and very large. It was a two bedroom with a nice size living room, dining room and kitchen. The kitchen was amazing actually. I was able to put a table and chairs in it. I loved it. One of the things that turned me on the most was that the master bedroom had two closets. One was typical size and the other one was a walk-in that was so large that it was more like another small room. I ended up turning that room into my meditation and prayer room. This was where I went when I felt any kind of stress coming on. I had tables set up in there with all my candles, tarot cards, Egyptian statues, incense, and a little radio that I could play my meditation music on. Aside from its intended purpose, I think that room also became something else. I think it opened up a door to another realm.

Once again things started to happen slowly. I never felt too much going on as far as people watching me. I never heard any voices nor did anything move. What I did notice was at night while in bed. Many nights I would wake up to a huge bubble floating right past my head into my meditation room. This would always make my heart race; I would sweat and just generally be taken off guard. Once I got a hold of myself I was not afraid of it but it did spook me upon wakening to it. This happened several times while I lived there. It seemed like they were spirits moving through or perhaps Angels. I was never really sure. These bubbles looked like soap bubbles almost only there were absolutely huge like a beach ball and they always whizzed right by my head. I felt like perhaps they were watching and protecting me. I could also always hear my son talking to someone in his crib. Now just to explain, my son barely talked as he has learning Autism so to hear him talking in his crib alone, you would have to think he was talking to someone in the room. Maybe it was his Guardian Angels. I would like to think so.

I also had a lot of strange dreams. I remember waking up one morning and clearly remembering that I had seen what I thought was as friend of mine with a flowing white gown on. She smiled at me and was looking at my jewelry sitting on the table. Oddly enough, my rings were neatly put in a row when I woke up. I sincerely thought that friend of mine had passed away and was visiting me through dreams but that particular friend is still alive. I do not know if maybe it was another spirit showing itself as a comforting image that I would accept or if it was an Angel that resembled my friend. Either way it was very strange and yet somehow beautiful. It always made me wonder what was trying to be communicated to me.

I was getting ready to go through a huge transition in my life and perhaps my Angels were being there for me to make my transition go smoothly for everyone involved. I certainly did my fair share of calling upon them for just that reason. They often calmed my stress and often gave me strength to get up and go. Things were not going well with my husband. I felt it was time for me to move on because I was tired of feeling the feelings I had. They were the typical woman scorned feelings and trying to force myself to feel for him what I was not feeling anymore and hadn't for years. I made a go of it just for the sake of our son but eventually I could not use that excuse anymore. I needed to be free. Life can be strange when you realize everything you knew was about to be gone and replaced by other things, people, places and thoughts.

If you ever feel that you are hurting so much, you long for change, you want more than anything to feel happy and full but you feel you are locked in, you are ***NOT***. Change is a very scary thin but it is in change that you grow spiritually. If you do not make changes as they come, you will not grow and you will become stagnant and unhappy. I implore you to ride with the winds of change when they come. Go with the flow.

Though all of the madness, I prayed a lot and I asked the Angels to surround me so that I would be protected. Every day I asked them to watch over me and my loved ones. Even though my changes would affect them, they would be protected as well to make the transition go smoothly as it can.

I knew that I needed to leave my situation as it was increasingly becoming more difficult. Every day I would wake up depressed and knew if I didn't do something about it, I might be stuck or end up in a hospital. It was that bad.

I was about to face yet another marriage ending. It was uncomfortable but I knew deep in my heart it was the right thing needed for us all. Sometimes the most painful of things are necessary to cleanse your heart and soul. What most people do not realize is that people come in and out of your life for a reason. Sometimes you think they are meant to be forever and then at some point your soul tries to tell you that it is time for them to move on and also time for you to move on. We all learn lessons from each other that are suppose to benefit us and help us to grow. It may seem like the farthest thing from beneficial until years later you think about it and realize it was for the best.

At the time I had a lot to consider and a lot to weigh out but either way I knew I needed to go. I had already been talking to a lot of friends who knew what was going on and how I felt. Of course at first they were only internet friends that I played an online game with frequently. But the time came to have a party with all of us members and so I set out on a trip by myself to go hang out with my friends. While there I had a lot of fun playing our games together and getting to know people face to face. I had an absolute blast and was reminded of how I should feel in life and how it wasn't lining up with how I had been feeling.

To add more to the pot, I had been talking more to one particular person more than the others. He was living about an hour away from where we were and did not have a ride and so I decided I would go pick him up. We went back and forth about it for awhile on the phone first and finally he agreed to let me. I told the gang what I was up to and they all wished me well.

I arrived at his house to pick him up and it was very late at night and he convinced me we should just wait until morning. We ended up watching a couple of movies and going to sleep for a couple of hours. No we did not do anything inappropriate. Just so I make myself perfectly clear, we were attracted to each other but we did not do anything we should not because it was not right for either of us. Everyone thought something was going to happen with us but it did not. I am not sure that people were convinced after the fact but that is neither hither nor thither. We were two adults with a decision to make and we did make the right one.

The next morning we drove back to the party and everyone was happy to see him. He was after all, one of the leaders of our gaming group. Shortly after we arrived I was told my ex kept calling the whole time I was gone. They kept making up things to tell him as to why I couldn't come to the phone. They should have just told him the truth. I would have been ok with that.

When I got back home things escalated, blew up, and I finally had reached my limit. I told him exactly how I felt and that I wanted it to be over. At first he went from being furious about thinking I had betrayed him to crying and begging me to not feel that way. It was a nasty scene of which I will not elaborate any further.

We lived together for a while until I could figure out where I was going to go. It was a very uncomfortable time as I wanted to be free and he wanted me to stay. He was convinced he could get me to change my mind and I swear if I had money at that moment, I would have left right then and there. Unfortunately I did not have that luxury. I did start talking to another gamer however. We began to get closer and closer and he understood what I was going through and offered for me to stay with him. I jumped on board with it. It was not the wisest thing to do as far as getting involved with someone but it was my way out and I felt confident it was the right opportunity I had been looking for.

I had not felt like this in a long time and so it seemed it was a great thing. I informed my ex that I was moving to Texas and that he would have to care for our son since I did not have the means to do it alone. The whole time I had been with him, I was a stay at home wife and mother. If I had taken my son with me, I would have had to have gotten on welfare and it would have been very hard on my son so I chose for him to stay put with his dad. I knew he would take good care of him. It was not easy at all to leave my son. There are times even now that I cry about it but I always know I did the right thing for HIM if not for anyone else.

I had to pack everything I could fit into my car which wasn't a lot because my car could not fit a lot. I fit my clothes, my computer, some dishes, some books, and some important things I had been carrying around since I was a teen.

I left in the early morning before it was light out. I knew I would just drive straight through instead of getting a hotel because I did not have money for gas and hotel, only gas. I stopped only when I needed gas and it was also when I would take opportunity to get something to drink and eat. It was about a 14 hour drive. I arrived in Houston around 6 or 7 p.m.

I had no idea what I was in store for. I had did not know how things would play out or where I would end up. This was a new beginning for me and it was both terrifying and exciting. I had big hopes and dreams that things would turn totally around for me. I wanted so much to be happy and be independent. I wanted to feel what it was like to live without oppression. Well, I was about to find out what my new life would bring and how it would change.

Chapter IV

Beginning of Change

In the midst of facing another marriage ending, I got the strength to get up and move on to the next scene of my life. It was scary and it was painful but it was what I needed to do. Granted the way that it happened was not what I considered to be the best way but it got me from point A to point B. Point B ended up being in Houston, Texas. I stayed with the man that offered me a place to live and a place in his life.

It was awkward from the start. This was a new place, a new person to adjust to and just in general, very scary. I didn't know what to do other than to go with it. He introduced me to his work friends at a picnic they were having that fall. Shortly after that I began working at the same little electronics store. We worked different hours sometimes and sometimes we worked the same hours so we could ride together. It was conveniently close to the house.

With time going by we realized it just wasn't going to work out for us. We were too different and we understood it was time to just move on. We both still continued to work at the same place and stayed friends. There was no reason to hold any animosity toward one another because nothing horrible ever happened between us. I had been disappointed when he would go out with friends and not invite me because at that point I knew no one so I had nowhere to go and no one to hang out with but that's the way the ball rolls sometimes.

I ended up acquiring my first credit card and moved into an efficiency apartment in the same complex. Oddly enough I currently live in the same complex as I write this book but in a larger unit. I have been here for an eternity it seems.

My efficiency was quaint and perfect for a single person to live in. It was just enough room and I had the place to myself. It was still close to work of course so there was no problem there. I practically lived on that credit card though until I ran the limit up. I was not making enough at my job to cover my living expenses let alone pay back the credit card. I was starting to face a significant amount of stress.

My car ended up getting repossessed as it was expensive as was the insurance for it. By the blessings of Angels, a customer of mine from my work was doing missionary work for his church and ended up giving me a wonderful little 1989 Honda Prelude SI. I loved it and it was very reliable. I had that car up until recently when I acquired my new baby, my 89 Supra.

When I first moved into the apartment I was super excited to have a fresh start again. I was learning what it was like to live alone. I never truly had done that before because even in my first apartment, I had people over all the time.

Everything was ok except for finances up until the holidays rolled around and I discovered I could not take off work to go see my family and they could not come to see me either. I was utterly alone during the holidays of my first year in my apartment. It was a very lonely experience.

After having had such a sad time happen, I decided I need to start to meet people so that I could have friends and not have a repeat of lonely holidays. I started putting myself out there on the internet. I joined forums, dating sites, MySpace, etc. I started to meet people with common interests after much effort. I started hanging out with people in the area and going out. I went clubbing, went to movies, dinner and other fun things. Finally I was having a life! Some of those friends, I still have today.

Going to a particular club time and time again, I got it in my mind to start helping promote it. It was a lot of fun and I got to be around my friends. The club appreciated the help as did my friends. Since it was working out well and I was help bring new people to the place, I decided to take it one step further after seeing a band play one night. I decided I would help promote them as well. So it was a combined effort and it was well worth it. They had cards that had the club on one side and their band on the other. I handed many of them out. A lot of my customers at the store were interested in what I was doing so it was nice to hand them a card and tell them to come check it out.

I did that for probably a year or so and then I started to go see the band play at other venues. In doing that, I met a lot of other bands and decided to expand my horizons. I quit going to the club as much and started going to various bars around town with the bands. They appreciated my promotions and my payment was getting into places for free, getting shirts, cd's and getting to hang out with them before and after shows as well as private parties. I was living the life of a rock star without the pay. The one thing I did not do is bring men home with me. When I was promoting, I was there to work. I knew that the guys there were drunk and only wanted one thing. I did not share in that and as such I did not drink much while promoting. I stuck to my guns, took lots of pictures of the bands while they played and did my job.

Back then I was still using the name "LadyBarker" because it stuck with me. I loved the name and everyone got to know me by it. Before I knew it many people in the industry knew who I was before I even met them. I had people walking up to me asking "aren't you LadyBarker?" It was the strangest feeling in the world. I felt almost like a celebrity. It was an amazing feeling. This was so much different from the life I was living before.

I was still working at the computer store and doing my promotions at night and weekends when I wasn't at work. The store closed at an early hour so that evenings were free. It was taking its toll on me though to be out late and getting up early in the morning to go work all day.

Not having friends was not a problem for me anymore. I had plenty of those to go around. I still felt lonely though when I would go back home to my apartment where no one was there to greet me. I felt like I had a void in me. I needed more. What could I do about it?

I started to go on dates here and there, nothing serious. But it would seem every time I would bring someone over that was of the male persuasion, something would always happen to them. They would tell me their shirt got tugged on, yanked, or they would get pushed. Some of them passed it off as nothing but some never returned because it made them nervous. I began to feel a presence there as well. Most of the time I could feel a male presence standing over by the sliding glass doors.

After a period of time going by with this happening, I sat down with a friend and the Ouija Board I had. We asked questions about what had been going on. This ghost told me his name, told me that he does not like any other men coming around because I belonged to him and he was not willing to share. He said he would protect me at all costs. At some point though, I had to put a stop to it. He was trying to sabotage anything I might have of value with another man. One day I just said out loud so he would hear me "you are dead, I cannot be with you so stop messing with the guys I bring around. If you care about me then you will want me to be happy and you cannot make me happy, please move on."

I do not think he moved on but I do think he let up and stopped messing with people. There were times though those things would happen that would make me think he was still there. I use to always shut the bathroom door at night so I didn't have to hear the neighbors. I would sometimes wake up and the door would be wide open again. He had to have left on his own at some point or maybe he stayed in that place after I left. He is not with me now so for that I am grateful.

I began to get very tired as sleep did not come often for me since I was working and promoting. At some point it began to get very old and so I made the decision to give up promoting. I figured out that being at the bars all the time whether promoting or not was just not my scene. The cigarette smoke thick in the air, the loudness, the groupies, the drunken men hitting on me, and just losing out on sleep from being up until 3 or 4a.m. I was literally exhausted.

I will say that one of my last promotion nights was with one of my girlfriends. She had invited a guy that she was sure I would hit it off with. You know what? I did. The next day I emailed him and then before I knew it, we were dating. He was different than the other guys I tried dating. He was very funny, very sweet, and I really just was taken by him. Unfortunately it didn't last long. He became afraid that I would hurt him and he also was very jealous by my male friends. He had no reason to be because I was happy with him and everyone knew it. Nonetheless he was afraid and he broke up with me. I thought I was going to die. It was one of the most emotionally painful things I had experienced. With my ex's things had died off over time so I had plenty of time to prepare myself for endings but this came out of left field and I knew I would never be the same. It took me a few years to get totally over it.

What could I do now that I was not promoting anymore? Well I went back onto my old friend, the internet. I was feeling that pull of feeling lonely again as all I did was go to work and come home. Now it is true that bars were not for me but it was also true that I did not know what to do with myself. I felt very complacent and worried that maybe that was all life was going to be for me. Maybe I was supposed to end up an old lady with a dozen cats in a one bedroom apartment. I would just go to work, come home and feed the cats. Ok so at the time I didn't have any cats. I had one Betta fish to come home to. A fish can only be so grateful for your arrival. The only thing they require is food and clean water.

I started trying to get back out there and went on some dates that were less than fun. Same type of guys out there on the dating sites, they want meaningful relationships until they meet you then all they want is sex and a goodbye. This was definitely not in my repertoire. I want what they claimed to have wanted. There are so many liars on the internet. If I had $20 for every liar I came in contact with via the internet, I'd be a rich woman now.

So back to my hum drum existence with a laugh here and there with a friend or a one night date without sex and without another phone call. I did meet one friend who did come around to hang out and watch movies. He did not want any more than friendship so I respected it and since I was in the market for friends, it sounded like a good idea.

One day I met someone who I started talking to quite a bit. He was a sweet guy, cute, and smart from what I could tell. It was through the internet again, yes. I had already taken chances but what the heck, thought I'd try again. This developed to talking on the phone for hours on end, constant chat on messengers, photos, and just general interest in one another. He was in the Navy at the time and was going through a lot where he was. I was able to help him through a lot of that hard time. Within a few months, he was out of the Navy and living with me. That was quite a journey for him all the way from Washington State to Texas. It was what he needed and at the time so did I. We had a lot in common and he was someone I could go home to and feel welcomed. Remember that people find each other to accomplish something and then they move on? Keep that in mind when I tell you this story.

He and I were pretty close but somewhere inside me I always knew this was not going to be a permanent thing. I wanted to feel forever though so I fought my gut feelings and moved forward. This was a hard lesson to learn. I know now that my gut is always right. Anyway, we married and after accumulating more things we were going to need a larger place to live so we moved to a large one bedroom unit in this same apartment complex. Before we moved out though, we started to experience a rise in paranormal events. We kept hearing things so one night we left a digital recorder going overnight. We listened the next morning and looked at each other like "what the hell?". We could clearly hear what sounded like a couple having a conversation in the living room. It was so low though you couldn't really make out anything they were saying. Then there were loud pops as if the couch was shifting because they were moving while talking. This was just too strange.

At this point I had decided I wanted to start a paranormal investigation group. So very quickly that is what we did. He would be our tech and I would be the leader. It started with just us two and shortly after we added another member who ended up being very sketchy so we let him go. While we were doing our dabbling with equipment and researching places to investigate, we were still having experiences at the house.

One night I was awakened to loud breathing in my right ear. Now he slept to the left of me and there was nothing to the right of me but the night stand with the alarm clock and a window. Right away I started in with logical reasons I was hearing this sound. Could it be the vaporizer? I looked over and it was unplugged! I then thought maybe the trash truck was passing in the neighborhood. Then I looked at the clock and it was only 3a.m. There was no way the garbage truck was passing at that hour. Right after that thought, the breathing got louder like it was frustrated that I was not listening. I got nervous and woke my husband up. I asked if he could hear what I was hearing and he said he could. As soon as he did, the breathing in my ear stopped. What was that?

On two other occasions I awoke to a little girl with a long white flowing nightgown standing at my computer messing around with my stuffed frog on the monitor and with my keyboard. The first time I saw her it startled me but she did not see me. The second time she did turn and noticed me. She started walking toward me and I gasped. She heard that and disappeared. I never saw her again after that. Who was she? Where did she come from? Did we bring her home on one of our trips to a haunted place or was she just passing through?

We started doing our investigations and on the very first night we got our first EVP. EVP is Electronic Voice Phenomena. It means it is a recording of voices that we could not hear with our own ears when we were at a place. These are known to be those of disembodied spirits attempting to communicate with us.

We went down this road that is said to be very haunted. People have things all over the internet about how if you stop on the bridge, turn your car off, and listen, that spirits will tap all over your car. We were determined to see if that was indeed the case. We tried it several times and the only conclusion we could come to is that people were hearing their cars cooling off which sounds very much like tapping. Also there are fairly large bugs out there that could be hitting up against the car in clumsy flight. We considered that to be debunked. We started walking up and down the road that first night with our recorder going and went over the footage after arriving home. We were so excited we listened to the whole thing right away and just as we were beginning to be disappointed by not getting anything, we hear a woman whimper. This whimper was very loud and distinct. You could tell it was definitely not me and of course it wasn't my husband. It was very much a woman weeping. We were just amazed and thrilled! We decided to return again later.

While we were doing this investigating, I quit my job and worked at another place for a few months. I ended up going to work at a place where I stayed for 2 years before being laid off. My stress levels were lowered as I was making plenty of money, my husband was working as well so everything was going great.

It was at this new job that I met my next member who also invited her boyfriend at the time so we now were up to 4 members. Things were getting exciting. We found other places to explore and invested in more equipment. I had my new members watch several DVD's of other groups so they could get a crash course in how to conduct a proper investigation. It was perfect! They were happy about it and began learning all they could.

In the midst of all of this excitement, my husband and I decided to go ahead and finally move. We moved into the large one bedroom unit and it was amazing and everything seemed perfect. The one thing that had not changed is that I still knew this was not going to work. That nagging feeling inside me would not let up. I kept fighting it though and kept moving forward. I was not ready yet to part ways.

Now there was a group to finally go do investigations just like I had always dreamt about. Another friend of mine ended up joining for a short while as well but her life had other plans so she ended up stepping down. We had all we needed to get moving.

We did return to that haunted road quite a few times and got many more EVP's. We also went to check out Poppet's Way. This place is known very well. There was a book written about it as well as a movie made. The location of this place is in Crosby, TX. There is a subdivision there that sits on the end of Poppets Way and Part Dr. The story goes that long ago there was a Plantation not too far from there. The owner released the slaves and gave them land to live on which is now this subdivision. The area where the two streets cross is where part of the cemetery was. The wooded area next to it is still intact for now. It is what is believed to be the other half of the cemetery. There are some very old trees there and the residents are happy to share the story with you. One man told us to look up at the trees for what would have been grave markers since the poor could not afford headstones. We tried to go out there during the day to see this, but the trees are just so tall there is no way to see them unless we would have scaled them.

The developers were going to bulldoze this area but the residents fought tooth and nail to keep it the way it is. They know the story and they are aware that some of them have graves below their houses and in their yards. As the book tells, one couple moved into what they thought was their dream home until all of these horrible paranormal things started to happen to them. We are talking about pets dying, family members becoming seriously ill, snakes constantly getting into the yard and house, and crows trying to attack them when they were trying to do some gardening in the back. There use to be an old tree in their backyard that had an arrow pointing down to the ground. Later they found out that it was a grave site for two sisters. While they were dealing with this, the neighbors also were having things happening. A couple of houses down from the main house of activity were another husband and wife trying to make their home more presentable. They decided to dig for a pool. When they did, they dug up a couple of caskets with skeletons in them. After that, no one dug anymore pools. That house still has its pool to this day but you can walk around and notice no one else does. Everyone living there now is aware of the atrocities that occurred there and so they are respectful.

After being armed with an arsenal of information we decided to tackle this place and see what we could get. We could not obtain permission to investigate homes so we decided to investigate the area itself and the woods next to it.

The first time we went out there, we got voices on our recorder as well as strange photos. This place was hopping with activity. My husband got touched and followed by a little girl ghost.

This was not the same ghost we saw in our apartment by the way. He kept feeling like a huge spider web was on his arm that he could not wipe off. At the same time he was feeling that, we got an eerie but sad EVP of a little girl saying "daddy, I want to see my mom" and it sounds as if she is crying at the end of the words. We walked around for quite awhile in the woods until we felt it was calming down. After we left and discovered our data, we were more than excited. We were absolutely thrilled! We knew we'd go back there again.

We did indeed go back to that place several times. One night we decided to split up so the guys went into the woods with the guy that lived in one of the houses there on the crossways of those two streets. He claimed to have had experiences in his home as well so he was intrigued to see what all we could get. We allowed him to because we figured it was ok and also it lets the neighbors know we were not there to destroy or vandalize anything. The neighbors actually became quite use to us and gave us their own stories. Eventually we put huge stickers on our cars so everyone knew who it was when they saw them.

In the woods, the guys started walking around and began to hear an extra set of footsteps around them. At first they thought it was an animal so they shrugged it off until the footsteps got more prominent and closer. They stopped and thought if it were an animal, if they threw a stick it would surely scare it off. They threw the stick and still the footsteps near them persisted. They had flashlights, so they could clearly see there was no living being there nor could they see a creature. In a bit of panic, they started walking faster and ended up getting turned around. They couldn't figure out which way was back to the neighborhood. They radioed to us girls to help them. We did indeed help guide them back out. After they walked out and told us what happened, I began clicking photos in the woods where they came out. I got a strange photo that appears to be a slave looking apparition peering around a tree.

While the guys were still in the woods, we two girls had been canvassing the neighborhood for any EVP's we could get. We did indeed get some that night! We had gotten one that sounded winded as though he had run to catch up with us to say "oh yeah, big deal". Later we sat on the curb for awhile and while we were talking a voice interjected on the recording. We couldn't make out what it was saying but it sounded like an old black man talking about something. It was shortly after we went to stand at the tree line to help the guys back out of the woods. Very strange and active night!

We were walking back toward the cars with the neighbor and we asked him about the cemetery that was supposedly not far from there. I said to him "so you said there is a cemetery nearby, where is it?" before he answered, on the recording we heard "this way" in a loud whisper. It was not faint, it was VERY loud and clear. Which way he was indicating, we are not sure. We did go walk down to where we thought it was and had even more weird things occur back there. It was a different part of the neighborhood that had another part of the same woods. We walked down the long shell road with the eerie woods on both sides of us. It was a very unnerving walk for sure. We got down there and could not figure out where to go next so we stayed local to that area without digging further into the woods. In that time we captured a couple of strange photos of strange lights touching the back of one of our members. There was nothing around there that could cause that nor did we have anything on us that would have ended up that way. Also one of the members started feeling ill so we decided to head out. She said that she felt like a kid was holding her hand as if to comfort her the whole way back to the car. She also claims it followed her and her boyfriend home that night and stayed with them for quite awhile in the house they were living in.

In time the two members decided that they wanted to get married and so they did. We attended their wedding and wished them well. They stayed apart of the group and we still went on investigations. In fact we returned to Poppets Way a few more times. The last three or four times we went though, it was very quiet and we did not get any activity at all. I have not personally been back since then.

The next place we decided to check out was Jefferson, TX. This place was an old railroad town. The whole entire town is haunted according to legend and townspeople. We were invited to stay in what use to be an old Tavern. It was a coffee shop last time we went and is now currently a sandwich shop. People still go there to investigate all the time. The door is always open to me whenever I choose to go out there. I am still very good friends with the owners.

Anyway, we set out on our journey to Jefferson. It was very exciting to travel away from Houston and to check out a new place. Unfortunately the downside was, it was a biker convention weekend also. There were huge bikes everywhere! It was so loud, at least most of the day and part of the evening. I think it didn't calm down until maybe 2 or 3a.m. We enjoyed walking around, getting dinner and site seeing for awhile until it got dark. We went upstairs and started setting up equipment. There was another team there with us that had invited us to investigate with them. We took them up on it. While things were being set up, we decided to go on the local ghost tour. It was very cool to walk around and hear the stories behind some of these historical places.

After the tour we returned to the coffee shop and headed back upstairs. We decided it was time to start trying to contact the spirits of the place. We asked a lot of questions, we played music from their era; we tried our best to get things to happen. There was a corner of the room that seemed a bit sad. Three of us tried sitting in that corner and all three of us started crying. We are not sure why that corner was like that but it was. Also just as one of the cameras was being changed out, there were three of us girls laying on the bed trying to get a reaction. Of course because we were not being filmed, one of our members was scratched and the bed fell at the same time. So we have a personal experience but no footage to back it up. That was frustrating to say the least.

In the early hours of the morning everyone started passing out. The other team had left to stay in a hotel. We wanted to stay there all night. I had just started to get drowsy since everyone else was already sleeping. All the sudden I hear loud footsteps enter into the room and across the hard wood floor. It sounded like boots. I looked up and around and saw absolutely nothing. There was no one there. If there had been, they would have been standing right in front of the bed. Unfortunately it was not recorded and I was the only one to hear it. But what is interesting is what happened after everyone woke up. Now reflecting back, I think what happened to me next was the same spirit that walked into the room.

A couple of hours later we all got up, packed our things, and went downstairs for coffee and something to eat. We talked to the owners and told them what happened overnight. They were a bit disappointed that nothing more happened. They have had so many experiences there as have other people who were either visiting or investigating. Apparently we had a very mild night compared to what it was typically like around there.

After breakfast and coffee we decided to go check out the Jefferson Cemetery. I started to notice very angry, jealous, sad, and vicious feeling. I kept thinking my husband was fooling around with my best friend who was there with us. I kept feeling like my other members knew and they were just not telling me. That is only a tip of the iceberg with how my feelings were going. This was not me and these were not my thoughts. I became aware that I was feeling and thinking someone else's thoughts but I didn't know what to do about it. As I was driving us all home, I was still very hostile. One of my friends tried to tell me something and I told them all to shut the hell up. They all decided it was best not to mess with me the rest of the trip. The traffic was adding to my aggravation and all I wanted to do was get home and lay down. That is exactly what I did.

Upon arriving home, I threw all the luggage and equipment off to the side and went directly to the bed. I slept for a couple of hours and when I woke up, I felt a million times better. All the feelings I had been feeling that were not my own, were gone. I couldn't believe what had happened because it had never happened to me before. Of all my years being around paranormal happenings and for it to just now get me. I wondered if I had done something different or had I been off my guard? I am not sure but whatever it was, it was very scary. I hope to never have a repeat of that.

Upon going over photos after that trip, I noticed there were several photos that I had not taken that were on my camera. I had been carrying it around throughout the cemetery and somehow the camera was taking photos on its own. They were creepy angled shots of certain areas in the cemetery. I have no idea what happened but I do know that my finger was not near the button that has to be pushed to take a photo. It also shuts itself off after a certain period of time of inactivity. I believe there were beings in that place that were walking around with us or it could have even been the one that was with me. For all I know, I might have done it without knowing. That is to say that maybe "she" took over me for a little while. The pictures didn't make sense though so I was sure that was not the case.

We listened to all of our audio and watched all the video. We got nothing reportable on either. Strange that most of our happenings were when the cameras and recorders were off. It's as if they did not want us to get them in action. I've found as an investigator though, most of them do not wish to be recorded. Some of them love it though. Some of them will go out of their way to interrupt your conversations. Those are the ones I find intriguing. It's as if they do not realize they are gone and want to take part in what you are talking about. They are intelligent but think they are still alive and well.

Chapter V

Bittersweet Passings

My group and I visited a few more cemeteries around Houston. We had a few interesting EVP's. The biggest thing was one cemetery we went to that sat back off a long wooded road. We had to park at a nearby neighborhood and walk to it. It was a very dark road because all the woods blocked the neighborhood lights as well as any moonlight. It's like you could look down the road and just barely make out light at the end but it was a long, creepy walk. Once we made it to the end of the road the field of graves opened up for a better look. There was the main portion with another trail through the woods that led to yet another section of the cemetery. One area was older than the other. Unfortunately there were many headstones crumbled due to vandals. There were also a lot of trees down and draped across the moonlit field. There was no doubt this place was different than any place we had already been. This place had a very eerie feel. We walked around slowly for a couple of hours doing our normal investigation of asking questions, hoping to get answers. We wrapped completely around the place, scouring each grave, each tree, and each statue.

Finally after coming back around to the entrance gate, we became restless and frustrated that nothing had happened yet. The two guys decide it's time to do some massive provoking. They start talking about possibly doing a rain dance on the graves.

A bit of history is that this area was in fact Native American territory and had been before anyone else moved into that area. There was a history behind it including battle and death. We did not figure that part out until after we had this experience.

It was on Halloween that we were trying out our provoking tactics in this hidden, moonlit cemetery off a long and creepy road. We were getting ready to leave after we made our last taunt when something stops us dead in our tracks. There were about 6 of us total and all of us froze and looked at each other. We heard what sounded like hundreds of Native Americans doing some sort of war call. They were yelling and screaming. We were all completely paralyzed yet scanning everywhere with our eyes. We didn't see anyone at the end of the road so we knew there wasn't anyone in that immediate area.

The noise finally stops and we decided it was time to go. We felt that we were wanted to leave so we did. As we were walking down the long road on our way back to the neighborhood, I look to my left to see one of my friends falling forward. I thought she tripped. She started walking faster than the rest of us. I looked at our other friend and asked if she saw what happened. No one saw it and the guys had just shut off the camera quite literally a minute beforehand. I walked faster to catch up with her and asked her if she was ok and if she tripped. She said she was not and she did not trip. She said she was shoved. She had taken the cue to get out of the area. We all followed suit and walked faster to get off that road. We were definitely not wanted around there any more for that evening.

It was a long drive that night. We were curious to go over our video footage to see if we had gotten anything and to verify what we were hearing. We had looked around the area where we parked to see if maybe there was a party going on just in case it was a bunch of people hollering out but there was absolutely nothing going on. We saw no wild dogs or anything else that could explain what we heard so we wanted to know if there was anything visible on video.

Looking over the video we did indeed capture the yelling and it sounded exactly the same as we heard it. It also came through loud and clear on our audio recorders. What was curious though was the apparition that was caught on our video. It was a white apparition that went quickly past the camera as the camera passed it. There was no one there but us and due to the moonlight lighting everything up nicely, we would have seen if someone were there. Was this figure a part of the sounds we were hearing or was it just there to watch our reactions? I do not know. Was it the one that pushed our friend? It is possible because it was heading in that direction, toward the road that is.

We went back to that place once or twice more, had nothing happen and then just forgot about it for awhile. When we did finally feel like going back again, we went down the road to find the place was totally fenced off with a security fence and a bunch of the woods were plowed down. It was very sad to see this. That place was so neat and creepy and now it lost some of its luster being more wide open to the public and closed off to us at the same time. They put a building there which I think may be for a caretaker or security. I would like to go check it out further sometime during the day where we can see what they have done with it.

We had to find more places to go. We were successful in doing that. The next place we went to check out was an abandoned hotel on top of a restaurant in Old Town Richmond. This whole town is like walking into a time warp. It is very old and very quaint. You feel like you are in the 1800's when you are there. I absolutely loved it. Jefferson was much the same. It's like getting out of the city and into a different time era for a night.

We were invited by some other friends of ours that also do investigations around Texas. They thought it would be neat to have us there with them to share some of the experiences they had at this place. The restaurant is alive and doing well but when you go upstairs, it is totally empty and of course just like any place like this, it has its own dark history. One of the stories is the guy that hung himself in one of the front rooms. Many people claim to see him from time to time staring out that window. We could feel sadness upon entering that room. Try as we did, we unfortunately did not get any evidence to show. We walked around the place for a couple of hours, tried several evp sessions and to no avail. Nothing unusual happened and we were a little disappointed. That is not to say that nothing ever happens there because our friends had plenty of experiences there. They just didn't have any while we were there.

Understand that just because I have had a lot of experiences in my lifetime, does not mean I walk into a place assuming what someone experienced is going to happen or is even valid. Another words I use a healthy dose of skepticism when I go to a new place. I will listen to all of the experiences people have had but I go into it with the mindset that there could have been other explanations for what they have experienced. Now if I have experiences and cannot find any way to de-bunk or explain them, then I will be more inclined to believe other people's experiences. I like to think that I try to be as scientific as I possibly can while doing an investigation. If things do happen that are paranormal, then I am thrilled but I do not want to work myself up in a frenzy based on someone's story of what happens there. That is when people can be tainted by fears they worked themselves up to have so the slightest sounds will have them believing there is nothing less than a ghost causing the phenomena.

There have actually been occasions where my team and I have debunked things. It is not that we enjoy de-bunking, it is more that we want to know if there is something really there or if something is causing people to be afraid when they need not be. We have done home investigations where we were able to show people what may have been happening and that gives them comfort in knowing there is nothing for them to truly be afraid of. So there is a very good reason to go into a situation with your eyes open but not tainted.

It took me a lot of trial and error to figure out that there is way too much room for human error as in mistaken information or vision. And there are of course sometimes clients that will say anything at all to try to get you to investigate their home that way they can tell all their friends they had Paranormal Investigators investigate their haunted home. It makes them popular on their block and with their friends. They may have nothing at all going on but now they are popular. The problem is, most of us think the same way when we investigate and so when the groups come out of those homes with nothing, what do they look like?

There are also people that fake their misfortunes such as scratches, bites, or anything physical they claim have happened to them. There is no way to prove it happened or it didn't if no one was around. All you have is their word. That is not much to go on if you ask me. I am not saying it does not happen. There are plenty of cases where it is very true. A vast majority of the claims though are not. You must realize that when someone comes back from a supposedly haunted room to find you and show you how they have been scratched, how sure are you that they did not do it themselves or that they did not run into something like a chair or something sharp sticking out? A person's word on this is all you have unless you have a camera rolling.

Talking about this makes me also want to tell you that this is exactly the reason why in my group, I insisted we stay in groups or pairs. A part of it is safety because some places you go into are not exactly rated for safety. There are a lot of abandoned buildings, cemeteries, etc. where you can hurt yourself so if you have someone else there, they can help you. But the biggest reason of all to have someone with you is validation. "Did you hear that?" Either a person can say they did or they did not but either way they were there for documentation purposes for when you are looking back over evidence. They can say they remember that moment and what was going on at the time. Certainly if you get scratched and someone is with you the whole time, there is more validity to your claim.

Clients do not know that is how we test things out and so they are excited to tell you that they were scratched, bit, or bruised. It is so important that if the client truly believes that they are having a serious problem in their home, do not pass them off as being nuts. Listen to what they say, write it down, document it, but do not ignore it. Later on if you have something happen to you in that same room the client did, it will help validate the client's claims as well as your own down the road. Remember we are trying to help them, not prove they are crazy. There are plenty of legitimate calls or emails you receive for help. If you go to their place once and get nothing then they call you a week later saying the activity kicked up, go back and check it out again. Do not leave these people hanging. These people would not call you if they did not feel you could help them in some way.

So as I said, go into cases and investigations with a healthy dose of skepticism. Listen to what they have to say, note it and then go see what you can find for yourself. I cannot stress that enough. Bringing anything you can to light will help. Always be prepared to take on the worst but prepare for nothing to happen. I know that sounds funny but if you think that way, you have a better chance of success.

Provoking is one of my favorite things to do. I will only provoke when we are getting nothing OR it is a very well known haunted place where people are known to get hurt by ghosts. I want them to hurt me physically so I can have it on film and document it and prove they were really there and really hurting people. With that said, once it does happen to me, I will be calling for reinforcements to help possibly remove these miscreants. No one should ever feel fear of getting hurt in their own home nor should they get hurt from walking through an old haunted building.

Am I afraid when I provoke? On some level yes I am. I am scared they may take me up on it and smack me. On the other hand if I get it on film or recorded then it was totally worth it. So I will talk all kinds of smack to try and get a rise out of these ghost villains.

There are times I use the nice route as well. I will try to entice a child ghost to play with me or talk to me. I will identify with a murder victim and tell them how much I understand their pain and that I want to help them.

Then there are times where I ignore them and pretend I am just there to have a good time. I'll talk to my partner and carry on a normal everyday conversation just to see if they will interject into our talk. That does sometimes work. Sometimes that is the best route if you are not getting any results. By pretending they are not there, they do not feel threatened and decide they can be comfortable with you being around.

Really what it comes down to is treating them as if they are still alive. How would you like to be treated? If you were a murder victim, what would you like to hear from people? If you were a lost child, what would they want to hear? What does a murdering convict expect to hear? Do what you think appeals in the situation.

I have been to some amazing places. One of the places I am referring to is The Stanley Hotel in Estes Park, CO. It was absolutely breath taking. It is a very huge and lovely resort hotel that harbors quite a few spirits that refuse to leave. After having stayed there for a weekend, I certainly understand why they would not want to leave. I did not want to leave that place either.

While investigating this beautiful piece of history, I joined with many other investigators on the same quest. We scoured everywhere we could and did what we investigators do. The most interesting things to happen were personal experiences. I am sad to say that there was no data on the video or audio devices. I did get a couple of temperature drops with the IR Thermometer though in my room. My husband at the time was with me and witnessed the temperature drops. I'd ask for specific numbers for it to drop to and it did just that. There was no air conditioning in the building and no draft in the area I was pointing the thermometer so I knew I was dealing with paranormal dealings.

I also used a pair of dowsing rods that I acquired from another friend there who is quite proficient with them. She has been doing them for years. In fact, we did a session with her and several other people in one of the most haunted rooms in the place. We got interesting answers for sure.

I got that someone followed me from the candy place down the hill by the shops. He wanted to see the hotel and so he hitchhiked with me. He liked the place. I never heard from him again after that session in my room.

The first night I was there, I sat down to get comfy on the bed and almost immediately felt a warm hand touch my inner thigh. How interesting that was! He did not do anything else but for a first time experience in this unique place, I felt I was home. I cannot explain but I feel as though I have been there before. It was comforting to be at The Stanley.

Second night there I had quite an experience. We had just gotten done doing a group tour and decided to walk up and down the hall on our floor. We all stayed on the fourth floor as it is said to be the most haunted. People on occasion would hear children running up and down the hall playing when there were no children in the building. We were walking right around the area where they have been heard and seen. Out of nowhere I keel over in horrible pain. My womb was on fire as if a red hot poker went into it. It was so bad my eyes got teary and I had to sit down immediately. I slid my back against the wall and down to the floor. My husband was there and was worried about what happened. I explained to him the feelings I had and how strange it was. After awhile he helped me up and slowly back to our room as I could not go on. I spent the rest of the evening in bed because this pain stayed with me for hours until it finally died off and did not return thankfully. I had not felt pain like that since my c-section when I had my son. This was intense. Later on we heard that there was a woman who either had a hard child birth there or had a miscarriage. I do not know if she touched me and so I felt her feelings or if the residual of it was there but it was odd that no matter how many times I had walked through that area, it was right then that I felt those feelings. I think maybe she wanted someone to share her pain with and I think I was the person. Maybe she picked up on my past and thought I could identify with her. I really am not sure but whatever the reason, it happened.

The next day we spent walking around and taking photos of the whole place. It was so beautiful and I was so sad to leave. It was one of those times where I wished I could make time stand still. Although I must admit that things were less than ideal between my husband and I. Everyone seemed to sense the tension and tried not to say anything about it until later when they found out that we were finished.

Yet we boarded that plane and came back to reality. It was time to get back to work and get back to normal day to day living. It was exactly what I was doing at this point, living day to day. It was time to go back to what life had to bring.

After several months of feeling like things weren't what they should be or needed to be my husband and I parted ways. Things had become too difficult to keep up and we really figured out we make much better friends than partners in life. Marriage actually tore us apart and drove a huge wedge between our closeness. We made a good go of it and for that I will never regret having spent the time we did together. We are still to this day, good friends. I wish him well on his journeys as I know he wishes me well. Not all relationships have to end horribly and hate brought about. I believe once you understand that not all people are meant to be in your life forever, you truly learn how to appreciate the time you had with the person and appreciate the lessons you learned from being together. It can be sort of beautiful when you think about it.

I will also tell you this. Whatever problems you have, you will keep facing them over and over in each relationship you have until you face them and make changes. If you think back and find that there is a pattern in your past relationship then you need to figure out what about you drew those experiences in. What is it that you need to change so that it does not repeat again? If you do not change it you will keep repeating your actions, you will draw in the same type of mate every time. Remember that when difficult people arise in your life, they are posing as a mirror for you. They will mirror your own actions. It will keep happening until you can actually see what it is they are doing that you typically have done in the past many times. Trust me once you figure it out, you definitely can see it all throughout your past. It is a jaw dropping experience. You start to re-evaluate who you are and who you have been. Once you start making changes though, you will notice that the universe will definitely welcome you with open arms and start making wonderful things happen for you. You will see many more people with a positive look entering in your life. I have found that when you are doing the right thing, making the right changes, etc. things start to really fall into place. I know in my life, the last year or so I have slowly started to draw in more and more spiritual people who are on a similar path and wish to share it with me. I feel very blessed to experience this. My changes came slowly over time and I am still working on them. It was not until after being with my last husband that I realized he was being a mirror for me. That was how he helped me. He taught me how to have more patience as well. But I learned more in the time after that which will be in an upcoming chapter.

Just please keep in mind that everyone plays a role in our lives whether it be positive or not. Either way it is always thought provoking and you have the power to change the experience you have. It is up to you how you handle it and how you live with it. There is always a choice even when you think there isn't. Sometimes not making a choice is a choice in itself. Start to see people for who they are.

Another gift I was blessed with was the ability to see right through people for their true nature. I can meet someone for the very first time and feel vibrations off of them. I can either feel that they are just fabulous people who are making the wrong choices, fabulous people making the right decisions, people that maybe once were good but have strayed from the path and decided to go down a very dark road, or just straight up people who are on the evil side of life and enjoy nothing but to destroy other people's lives. Yes I can actually feel these vibrations off of people. It has been very helpful to me in the past and I hope it keeps going in the future.

I have avoided some grave situations by choosing to never be around a person who I felt bad vibrations about. I have told ex's to get rid of someone or to never bring them into our home again only to find out later those people ended up in jail or worse. I trust my vibes when I feel them when it concerns something so important like this.

How do you do this? It's simple really. All you need to do is feel your gut feeling. If right off the bat unsure about someone, go with it. Nine times out of ten you will be correct. It may not seem that way for awhile, you might feel you were being judgmental or just plain mean but trust me when I tell you that people like this pretend to be the nicest people on the planet because it is easy to pull you in that way.

So the first thing you feel, the first thing that pops in your mind, is your gut talking to you. You can ignore it if you want to but I promise you it will not end up being a nice scenario. I have tried to ignore mine with people before but I always ended up disappointed. You can weed out people for dating purposes this way too. If you feel the word "player" comes to mind, for goodness sakes, believe it! We are all psychically equipped to know these things. If you ignore it, go out with them anyway, what happens typically? You get hurt because they are not interested in holding a one on one relationship or at least not for long.

I can honestly say I did not follow my gut on many occasions as far as dating but for me, I chose not to listen to my intuition because the loneliness was much more pressing. I am not saying that it's ok to allow that to happen. If you can possibly avoid it, do not buy into anything just for the sake of not being alone. What is worse, being alone or being with someone who does not really want to be with you and ends up hurting you? Honestly when this happens you have no one to blame but yourself. Those people are who they are and you chose to ignore it. I am not excusing their behavior either so please understand that what I am trying to tell you here is to not put yourself in that situation if you can possibly avoid it. Trust your gut people!

If things do not feel right then most likely they are not. This is taught in many Eastern Philosophies. Most of them all rely on the feelings you have. If you feel that someone is a bad person there is likely to be a darn good reason behind it and if you continue to be around them despite what your feelings have told you, then you are in for a nasty wake up call. There are also people that are kind of in the grey area. What I mean is that they seem so nice, say all the right things and then later you find out they were lying the whole time and doing an excellent acting job. Those are unfortunately people that you will not know their true colors until you have spent a great deal of time with them. Of course that could also mean they are there to mirror you. Another words they are there to bring up something you need to face and get past in your own life. They will do exactly what you are normally the one that does. It will make you realize how bad it makes you feel when it is done to you so that later on when they are gone, you can make changes and not be who you were before they came along. This is a part of what I believe. Remember those people who come into your life to help you learn? These are those kinds of people.

Please just listen to what you feel inside when you meet someone. If you are the type of person that gives everyone a benefit of the doubt without trusting your instincts then perhaps you are also the type of person who ends up playing martyr or victim. Either that or you are just so giving of a person that you try to believe everyone is good and pure of heart. That is lovely but in the end I guess you end up learning they are not all that way.

Try this exercise and see how it works out for you. The next time you meet someone for the first time, see what the first thought that pops in your mind in terms of good, bad, grey area. Go with it and see what happens. It is such a useful tool to use. In relation to the paranormal, you can also sense what is good and what is not when you feel a presence around. When you know it's not an evil presence, you will feel calm and at ease enough to ask questions and relate to them. Give it a try!

Chapter VI

What dreams do come

Have you ever had a dream that seemed so incredibly real that when you woke up you could still smell, taste or feel what you were experiencing? You awake feeling like it was not really a dream? From all my years of experiencing this, I have found that I have actually been Astral Travelling without conscious awareness of doing it. For a large portion of my life up to even now, I have these dreams periodically that feel so real that I wake up exhausted. Most of them revolve around the paranormal. Now please keep in mind, I am not that afraid of the paranormal but these dreams I have are just so horrible, they make me so scared I wake up shaking and have to take a few moments to make sure I stay awake as to not immediately enter back into the dream.

These dreams feel more like someone is pulling me into their reality to help them. Usually it is a ghost amongst several others who are trying to get away from a malevolent spirit who keeps them captive and tortures them. I get there, walk around completely bewildered and begin to experience some extreme activity. Things flying at me, moving around the room, walking, pounding and suddenly the spirit that pulled me in insists I help them to break free of the tyrant. So here I am running around with these disembodied souls trying to outrun a larger and much more powerful entity. It's always the same, they want to be free. I always fight for them in any way I know how and by the time I am done, I awake from my dream and I felt as though I had been running a marathon. My body feels exactly the way I felt in the dream and somehow I know that it wasn't just a dream. I feel as though I keep being pulled into another realm to help those who cannot seem to help themselves. It doesn't happen very often. In fact, I haven't had it happen in over a year.

The last known experience I had was a couple of years ago in which I was meeting with someone on another plane for a couple of months straight. Once I lost communication with the person on this plane, the travels ended. It was confirmed by a psychic who knew nothing about me that I was doing this. When I asked if it was who I thought it was, without mentioning names, she said yes you most definitely were connecting. Since I lost connection with this person I cannot confirm it from that side. All I know is that it was very real and when I woke up from these dreams, I could still feel what I felt, smelled what I smelled and knew that it was not just a dream.

Many people are aware of their own Astral Travel and can even control it. They can go see who they want and where they want. I have not been fortunate enough to develop these abilities. I do not know how to relax enough to send myself somewhere. Your spirit literally lifts up out of your body and goes. I personally know people who have control over this. It's an amazing gift to have. I think we all have it but I think we all sort of let our everyday lives control most of our thoughts and end up pushing out the gifts we were given.

Can you imagine what it would be like to just leave your body and go see your loved ones? You can see friends, family, and long lost people from your past. You can see what they are up to, how they are doing and even sometimes what they are doing. There are always people I wonder about and wonder what they are doing with their lives.

Another interesting thing about dreams themselves is that they can actually give you information to your deepest questions. We do possess all the knowledge we ever truly need within and it is up to us to access it. For me, I ask Archangel Michael to guide my dreams to help me with answers and help to remember my dreams once I wake up.

It is incredible the amount of information you can truly pull from your dreams. Most of my dreams give me the knowledge of what is coming up and what my choices will be. The thing that is the hardest though is interpreting the information being given. You may have some crazy dream that you were on a train and people were chasing you. No matter what you did you could not get rid of them until you stop and ask them what their problem is and what they want. Something like that would be interpreted as you cannot keep running from your problems, face them head on and you will get the answers you need. That seems simple enough right? Then you could have some crazier dream that you are flying and suddenly land in a zoo where all the animals are happy to see you but the zookeeper wants to kill you. Who knows what that could mean? Not all dreams are easy to figure out. I think sometimes we dream of things we want, things we need, things we lack, things that will happen, and things we fear will happen.

I use to have a reoccurring dream about my mother being taken away in a dumpster by the trash men. Every time I would wake up, I would look to see if my mother was still there. As you know, she worked a lot so whatever time I had with her was very valuable. I was always afraid of her disappearing out of my life for good. Thank goodness that never happened but you can see how my fears manifested themselves in my dreams.

To this day I still periodically have this dream where I wake up in a huge mansion that is incredibly haunted. I am trying to gather data and suddenly things go horribly wrong and I am looking for a way to get out of there. They begin chasing me all over the place. I end up getting out of the house via the basement that went back up a few steps to the outside. After I run outside, they start following me and I am left running from them outdoors and I wake up. I do not know whose house this is, where it is or any of that information but I do know that it has everything to do with my love for paranormal investigation. There are times that even I fear something or several some things following me home. I would be willing to bet that almost all investigators feel that way at some point in time.

Dreams are crazy things but dreams can be wonderful things too. Sometimes you can dream of things like seeing your soul mate or seeing dead loved ones. Dead loved ones do visit you in your dreams. They appear the way you remember them as to help you feel comfortable. They tell you how much they miss you, love you, or even to warn you about something coming up. That is always a beautiful thought, to think of your loved ones being just a dream away. It is very true though. I remember going through some hard times in the past and someone who I loved very much use to visit me in my dreams, hold me and tell me everything was going to be ok. I would wake up feeling better. There is nothing like a boost from the other side to make you feel better again.

Dreams can also alert you to things going on in a much larger scale. I clearly remember dreaming one morning. I was seeing me being with my family and driving across a bridge in what appeared to be New York. The skies became very dark, I saw fire and I saw three buildings collapse. I remember how sad and devastated we all felt. I woke up feeling saddened and glad that I was awake. Shortly after I woke up, I went and turned the TV. on only to find the plane crashing into the second tower in the horrible 9/11 event.

With such tragedies such as 9/11, I believe that it touched most of us on a very deep level. It showed just how connected we really are as human beings. Almost everyone I knew was deeply upset and saddened by this event. Most of us actually went so far as to be depressed about it. Those of us who did not have family there were still grieving those lost as if they were. It was such a huge impact on humanity. It made us all rise up and do everything we could to try to put things back together again.

Years later some of us still remember but life has gone back to business as usual. Why does it take such a horrible tragedy to get people's attention and to remember that we are all connected? Why is it so important to cut someone off in traffic? Do you forget that they are your connection? Traffic is just one example. I can think of a lot of other things that show that people have gone back to being self absorbed and worried about only their lives. It is really sad when you think about it.

If all of us could get back to that connection and live that way, this world would be a better place. Unfortunately I believe that most of us chose our paths and living in harmony may have not been the path we chose. And then some of us are here to battle the urges to separate from humanity and try to re-unite everyone as best we know how.

Why am I bringing up dreams in this book? Well it is important and it does involve the paranormal. It does in fact, involve everything and everyone. Just because someone has died and their ghost is still here does not mean they are any less apart of us. If we can understand why they chose the way they did and even try to help them, we are helping humanity. It is just another field of study to help those in need. It is one more step toward figuring out what we can do as human beings to live in harmony and perhaps prevent people from being so distraught that they choose to stay here in spirit form.

When I die, I want to move on to the next place I am meant to go. I have no desire to linger around this dimension and watch my loved ones grow old and die. I do not have more life I feel I need to live after I pass and I do pray that an untimely death does not trap me to being here without me realizing it happened. I do not wish that on anyone.

Where do we go when we die? No one really knows the answer to that question fully until we get there but what we do need to know is that we should strive to be better human beings until it is our time to move to the next level and the next place. If we spend so much time worrying about where we are going then we don't enjoy what we are living right now in this moment. It is so crucial to live every moment we can while we are still alive so that when we do die, we are fully ready for the next step.

I do not believe that when we die it's over. I don't believe we are just shells that get put in the earth to feed the animals only. I believe very much that we leave these bodies, these shells, then we move on to a new place and move on to new things and people. There has to be more than just live and becoming part of the Earth again.

We are all elevated beings and it is time we start living this reality. This does include living by humanity, not by what someone thinks you should live. Do you know in your heart what is good? Do it! Do you know in your life what feels bad or isn't good? Then don't do it. It's really that simple.

If you pay attention to your dreams, they will give you all this information. If you do not know how to delve into this, there are a lot of books out there to help you interpret them and also ways to train your mind to answer your questions. Please believe that the answers are in you.

All of this sort of integrates with things I went through and still go through in my life. After three marriages gone wrong, I started to evaluate what the problem was. I found that I married for the wrong reasons and not one of them was from real true love which is what marriage is suppose to be. It is suppose to be a special and holy bond between two people who choose to stay together the rest of their lives.

The problem with that belief is that how to you know for sure the person you are with is suppose to be the one to stay with you the rest of your life? Therein lies the problem! From my experience, it always feels so good at the beginning of the relationship. It feels romantic, you cannot stop thinking of the person, and you cannot wait to see them or hear their voice again. It's like when you had a school kid crush only as an adult you think because you are mature, it will last forever.

Where it starts to clue you in is when you actually start noticing red flags that unfortunately a lot of us ignore in the sake of wanting to be right and the truth b so wrong. Once again, dreams kick in and start to tell you the truth but again, we want to be right. We want to make it so that this person IS the right one. There is something to be said for stubbornness.

Dreams can tell you flat out when something is not right. You start to have dreams that you catch your lover cheating or you start dreaming about fighting with your mate. The dreams seem so real you wake up still upset and it starts things in motion. You try to pass them off as just dreams but in reality, there is something very deep on a subconscious level you are ignoring. You find you start to dream about other mates from the past or people you do not know that are very drawn to in your dream. You wake up confused and not sure of what to make of it. You will also notice it starts sowing the seeds of doubt. This isn't just your imagination folks. Your own subconscious mind is trying desperately to reach out to your conscious mind. This is one of the ways our inner awareness tries to guide us.

Our minds are an amazing tool for guidance and intelligence. It is our conscious mind that needs to listen more to our subconscious mind. That part is very difficult and without proper guidance can cause us to have many problems throughout our lives. We need to be more in tune with ourselves and the world around us like we did during 9/11. We need to always live as if your neighbor is your family. If we could all rise up like this we could change so much for the better of the world. I implore you to read as much as you can on opening up your mind and learning to use your hidden gifts. You have it within you to change so much.

Pay attention to your dreams from now on. Keep yourself a journal next to your bed and start writing down what you dream. You will notice when you go back and read the notes how much info you were actually given. If you need help there are plenty of Dream Interpretation books out there that can help point you in the right direction. There are also plenty of meditations you can do that can help you as well. Meditation is basically like a dream state while you are still technically awake. You are in such a state of relaxation you can receive messages easier and gain peace of mind in an otherwise stressful life. Doctors are now backing up the fact that people should meditate for their health. When you are in deep relaxation your body is able to heal itself better and just generally puts you in a better state of mind.

Deep breathing is my favorite form of meditation. I have a very hard time quieting my mind enough to try to have an elaborate meditation. It is actually easier to listen to very calming music without singing and focus on being underwater, laying in the sun, or focusing on a color. I was told by a professional that the best way is to meditate without doing anything in it. He said that when you are doing something in your meditation, you are not fully relaxing. So just imagine something you really like and imagine you are just sitting there or laying there enjoying what you are looking at. When you come out of this state you feel completely relaxed and ready to get through the rest of your day. We all should be doing this at least once a day. I have the habit of putting it off if I do not feel good. That is precisely when you should do it!

Not too long ago I went for Kinetic Chromo therapy and Reflexology. I did this because I knew my chakras were out of whack and I needed to get them in line again and to distress. When he massaged my feet he told me that I do not relax enough. He is actually the one that gave me the info on the best way to meditate. He said that my meditating while doing Yoga was not going to cut it. He said to fully relax you have to actively do nothing at all. He also said that if I do not do it, I would never be in tune enough to fully experience and hear everything that the spirits want to tell me. He said I could absolutely forget hearing from the ghosts unless I do the work and get back in tune. He was right. I went on a trip, which I will talk about later, and I did not get the results I had really hoped for. It was very eye opening and disappointing to say the least. I did gather some cool evidence but not like what I could have.

I am sharing all this information in the middle of my story to let you understand the importance of these things. I have had to learn the hard way because that is the way I chose it to be from before I came to this Earth. I chose to take the harder road rather than the easy way. The reason is because going the hard way helps you to learn that much more and faster. If everything is handed to you, it takes you longer to learn your life lessons. Now I am trying to save you as much stress as I can but ultimately it is always your choice in what you will decide to do with the information I give you. It is always nice to know there are others out there that feel this way and are experiencing these things.

Also as an investigator, it is important to go into it as fully armed as you can if that is what you choose to do. I am guessing though, if you are reading this then you must be either interested in the paranormal and possibly even want to become an investigator yourself. Maybe you are psychic and do not know what to do with it or how to help others with it. Either way, I am here to tell you everything that I know.

In the next chapters I will wrap up my personal life and also help expand on what you can do to become a paranormal investigator. I will tell you the way you can go about it, who to talk to, what tools to use. I want to make sure you get the most out of my book..

Chapter VII

Reviving Again

After another ending I had to figure out how to start over again. I was still working at the same place and still maintaining my group. We had slowed down considerably though due to our jobs and personal lives. I had begun talking to someone who had worked for the same company a couple of years before. Unbeknownst to me, he liked me the whole time. I decided to see where things would go with us. At the time he was in Chicago doing some electrical work for a friend in a Halloween haunted house. It was very clear that he wanted a relationship and I thought I would like to also give it a try. He was in Chicago for about a month and a half before he came back home. We never really gave it time to grow and immediately moved in together. He moved in with me into the apartment I was already living in because it was convenient. I wanted him here and he wanted to be here. Things were great. We were very close and it felt right to be together. He used to drive me to work and pick me up. I had my own car but it was more romantic to do it that way. There were times he would pick me up a cup of coffee and bring it to me on my break time. I could not imagine things being any better.

I heard of an investigation coming up in Yorktown, TX at an old closed down hospital. A large group of my friends, the same from The Stanley, were going to be holding an event. I quickly signed my group up for it. I just knew it was what we needed because we hadn't been on an investigation in awhile. These types of events cost money of course. I have yet to go to an event and not have to pay. These people that run these attractions charge for people to investigate and they use that money to keep those places operational so that people like us can go an investigate. It all works out for everyone involved. Unfortunately that also means that a large portion of us can only go to one or two of these events in a year. Some are blessed to go as often as the events arise. I hope to someday be able to do the same.

The time grew near and it was time to pay for this event. We knew we would drive home from Yorktown since it was only a couple hours drive. I had signed up for a handful of us to go and only four of us ended up going. Some of the members had other things going on that weekend so they were unable to attend. These things happen in a group. Not everyone will be able to attend every investigation because we all have lives outside of the group.

I asked my boyfriend to join our group and he agreed. I thought he could contribute to our equipment collection as far as creating new things that no one in the industry had yet. He wanted to see what we do so he could figure out how to make equipment for us. He's a brilliant Electrical Engineer so I believed he had a lot to offer a group like ours.

The night of the event, us four drove out to Yorktown and met up with the larger group and we socialized for about an hour before everyone else got there and we began to do our walk through. They wanted to show us the place and give us the story behind it before letting us go on our own. This place was very dark and very creepy. It was indeed what you would expect in an old hospital. It also had a chapel that was lit up with candles. I think they were letting it be a safe room of sorts. We walked up and down these halls and then to the basement. The basement was pitch black and when you turn all lights off; you cannot see a hand in front of your face. It was just that dark. It was very creepy and started to add to the evening to come.

After the walkthrough we were broken up into groups. We had so many people breaking into groups was the only way to do this. We got in our groups and began walking to the areas we were assigned first. We were the main floor and to the East Wing of the hospital. This whole place was very interesting and in certain areas I could definitely feel things but I am not sure what it was I was feeling. I could have been feeling left over energy from the past or it could have been energy off of my fellow investigators. Whatever it was, I could not pin point. We walked around for a couple of hours in the hospital with our cameras rolling, I.C. recorders for recording spirit voices, K-II EMF detector, and digital cameras. We tried with all our might to get the supposed spirits to talk to us, move things, or touch us.

We went upstairs which was the Nun's area. The whole floor was where the Nuns stayed when they were off duty from the hospital. We had heard stories about a man that lurked in the library that did not like women. We've heard of women getting scratched and pinched when they were in the library. I was all amped and ready to give my all in this room. We sat in there for almost an hour and I provoked as hard as I could. I called this guy names, told him to knock me on my rear end and told him he was lame. As scared as the other people with us were when I as doing this, they still chuckled with some of the things I said. I am sad to say that absolutely nothing happened. I do not know if he just wanted nothing to do with me or if there just wasn't a ghost there at all. We debunked a few things as went along. We figured out how a particular door would slam and why.

In the Maternity wing, I felt totally creeped out. I felt like someone was watching us and following us however; we did not hear or see anything at all. I think that the stories of babies crying could have very easily been a cat wailing outside. We did in fact hear a cat outside in heat bellowing. It sounded very much like a baby cry. The other thing was, there were a lot of open windows and even broken windows so we could hear a whole lot of what was going on outside. There was a party going on down the street and people peeling out in their cars. It was very distracting and any of those noises pollute any data you can possibly get.

Now we had heard several stories about this place and I certainly will not sit here and tell you they are all lying. I do not know if they truly experienced these things or not but I can tell you that we found logical explanations for most of the things that were claimed. This does not mean we debunked those people. People can very much have personal experiences that we may not be able to debunk. Unfortunately the night we explored, we did not get anything on our recorders or cameras.

After we got done with the Library area, another group went in and said they got a lot of activity. They were able to get the ghost to knock on things to give them a response. I do not know if I got the ghost all full of energy or if it didn't like me but liked them. I am not sure what happened or if what they experienced couldn't be explained. I was envious though that they were having activity after we had hours of nothing.

The place was very cool and very creepy. I would go back just to explore but I would have to say I will probably not return for an investigation. I believe our findings showed there was nothing there but you know, I could be very wrong and I would love to hear more experiences from more people. Maybe it would inspire me to change my mind.

After investigating this place we were back home and had to figure out more ways to investigate other places. Just so happened one of our member's had a grandmother who claimed that her and her husband thought their place may have some ghosts. We told them we'd do an investigation for them. We sat down with them and had a battery of questions. We recorded the whole thing and took notes. When we did our actual investigation we asked the clients to leave the house so we could conduct a full scale investigation. They agreed and left us to our work.

We did our set up and tackled the areas that were supposedly the most haunted or had the most activity. Unfortunately again, we came away with nothing. We had nothing on our cameras or recorders to show for anything. This is not to say that their house never has activity but there was nothing going on that night.

I believe that people have experiences when there are earthbound spirits around. The thing is, you can have activity on and off and your house not be haunted. I believe this was one of those cases. As I have been learning, these earthbound spirits feed off of our energy to live so they will go where they think that they will get what they need. They may latch on to a particular person who reacts to things drastically so that they can feed off of them after scaring them. Again, this does not make the house or the person haunted. It just means at that particular moment, they have had an encounter with a ghost. It may come back or it may leave and move on to another place or person. I have read that they tend to go to places with more people such as bars, parties, restaurants, sporting events, and basically where there is a lot of excitement so they can feed off of the energy being passed around by the living.

That having been said, we have investigated quite a few cemeteries and typically didn't get much activity at all. There is not really a reason why we would. A cemetery is the quietest place for the living and the dead so they have no reason to be there. Now I have heard they do attend funerals so this is not surprising. Apparently the only time they visit a cemetery is either because they followed the living there or they are going to check their burial plot for whatever reason. Most of the time though, there isn't a spirit lingering.

That having been said there is a cemetery not too far from here that used to have quite a bit of activity. I believe it was because of the number of investigative teams that went there. I believe the spirits were feeding off of their fear and excitement. People would get touched; clothing pulled on, and talked to. We did actually get a voice in that area one time. But nine times out of ten we got nothing from the place. We do not know if it died down because the area became more open to the road and more trees were torn down or if they just decided enough was enough and moved on. Either way we were getting nothing and have not gone back to that place since.

After a few more small investigations and a lot of other personal issues going on with each of us I decided it was time to retire the group. It was not going the way I had dreamed of it going and I thought maybe it would be better if I just started attending investigations all over the country with other groups and people. The group thing had become a very straining and confining situation. After I disbanded the group the other two main members decided to start their own group. They are still friends of mine and I wish them well. They have a lot of opportunities ahead of them for a wonderful life. I hope their group pans out for them as well.

My boyfriend and I kept going with things and then May rolled around. There were a lot of lay-offs going around the city due to the decline in the economy. I became increasingly worried about my job. His seemed fairly secure as it was a small company. My job however was not a critical part of the company I was at. I was asked to start training a couple of other administrators how I do things. I was told that it was just in case I needed to call in or go on vacation so that everything would be covered and no one would have to worry. I somehow had the feeling though that I was training others so they could lay me off. That is exactly what happened a month or two after I did the training. There were several employees that got the boot at the same time I did. A week later they let another large group of people go. I hear they are still working but have not begun hiring anyone back as of yet.

After feeling the stress of being unemployed I had to start figuring out my life again. My boyfriend insisted I take time off before trying to return to working. He said I needed to live for awhile first to really experience what life could be. I appreciated that but unfortunately I became incredibly depressed instead. I had been trying not to take things personally but I really did. I felt like they had other administrators to choose from that had been there a lot less time than I had but yet I was the one chosen to go. I had been lied to when I was told that the managers spoke highly of me. I do not know if that is true or not but it was certainly how I felt.

After several months of depression I was forced by a possible ending of my relationship, to wake up and get moving again. I started getting out and doing things as well as hanging out with friends again. I started reading motivational books and really got back on life. I was still not working as I was still hearing how bad the economy is and how hard it is out there to find a job. I did at one point send out several resumes to companies but never got responses so I gave up. I figured out it was just a bad time to try to get employment when there are thousands also trying to do the same thing. It is like a war out there to get a job these days. They have thousands applying for the same positions and have plenty to choose from. It really does make one feel inadequate. Some places you are over qualified and some places you are under qualified. Where do you go? It's very hard out there right now.

Amongst all of this going on I heard of an amazing event going on in June of 2010. I signed up and scraped all of my money together to go. It was with a very famous group and it was for everyone. There were approximately two hundred people that showed up to this event plus the several celebrities that were there. We were going to investigate Eastern State Penitentiary in Philadelphia, PA. This was very exciting. I paid months in advanced so I had much excitement building over that time.

After I ended my group, my boyfriend decided he wanted nothing to do with the paranormal anymore. He is a science mind and does not believe in any of this. He said he cannot be a part of something he does not believe in. So I was now totally into this adventure by myself. I was going on this trip alone. I was both scared and excited. I would have to fly alone and get a hotel alone. I had never done this before.

I have several piece of equipment that I brought with me. I have a nice Sony handy-cam with night shot built in. I also have an extra IR Illuminator that powers off of a homemade battery pack that my boyfriend made for me so that way it would run all night. I have a few extra batteries for my camera so that I could switch them out when they got too low. I also have my K-II meter as well as my IC Recorder. I was completely armed and ready to go on this trip! I knew I would be running all of the equipment alone since I no longer had a group. I bought myself a pair of Capri pants with numerous large pockets so I could put my batteries in. I had my K-II velcro'd to my IC Recorder that went in one hand and I held my video camera in the other hand with my extra battery pack in a carrier that attached to my belt. I was a one woman show.

Since right before the birth of my group I began networking on my websites. I created a website for the group and had plenty of other resources to be connected to as well. To this day I still have all of those contacts and remain very close friends with some huge names in the industry. I now have my own website rather than the group and still maintain the social networking sites as to stay in touch and stay informed with things going on. I learn about the latest and greatest devices to use out in the field as well as new and upcoming groups. It's all fascinating to me. I own DVD's that I either bought or my friends sent me that I like to review to see how they do their investigations. I think it's always good to get different perspectives. If you always do things the same way how do you know that another way might not be more effective? It is also helpful to know how people work before you go on an investigation with them. Being armed with data is a very good thing.

I kept in contact with several people who would also be there to enjoy their first time investigating. Many of them had become interested after seeing this famous group do their thing. Basically they were fans who wanted to know what it is like to actually do it themselves. A lot of those people I am happy to say are now my friends after having met and spent time together. They are wonderful people and I cannot wait to spend more time with them.

After all of the build of excitement the day finally arrived and it was time for me to go on my adventure by myself and end up with other people on their own adventures. I boarded the plane with anticipation. Unfortunately it was a bad way to find out that I tend to get motion sickness. It was the first time I had ever vomited on the plane. Good thing they put barf bags in the seat pocket in front of you. I was so excited that by the time the plane landed it no longer mattered that I had been sick through the whole three and a half hour flight. I knew a couple of my friends were already there waiting for me to arrive so we could then meet and greet another one of our friends flying in after me.

After gathering up, we took a shuttle to our hotel where we would all be staying. We couldn't check in right away but while we were in line waiting a couple of the celebrities were walking around the hotel. Both of them recognized me and called me out by name. After all they were not just celebrities they were my friends that I had networked from the time they were first heard of. They gave me hugs and then they went about greeting the other guests. Eventually we ended up upstairs in line to register for the event and receive our badges to wear throughout the weekend. It was a very long line and a very long wait but we had good laughs and met other people in line that we knew online as well. Our friendship circle seemed to grow very fast and we took a lot of photos.

We finally got our turn to register and receive our badges. We got to say hello to other celebrities while were there and then a few hours later after dinner, we were able to attend the official "Meet and Greet". We all stood in line, took photos, got autographed photos, bought t-shirts, etc. It was a very good time.

Later after everything was said and done my group of friends and I went down to the pub located inside the hotel, shortly after the guys all joined us and partied with us the rest of the evening. I had an absolute blast with all of my friends.

The next day we attended all of the seminars the other known names had to offer and then because we were divided into two groups of one hundred, our group went to Eastern State Penitentiary on Friday night. We all chose the same night so we could stay together. We were given an hour or so to get our stuff ready and head to the front of the building to take the bus over to our destination.

I was so excited I didn't know what to do with myself. I almost forgot things in the hotel room. I think I went back two or three times after walking out of my door to go grab things or put something back. I got downstairs and got in line with my friends to wait for boarding the bus. We all laughed a lot and took more photos.

Finally we arrive at Eastern State Penitentiary and I am just floored by the size of it from the outside. It is absolutely huge. I have seen several photos and seen several shows where people investigated it but I still did not realize how huge it actually was until that moment. It was amazing and the style of building was very gothic and lovely.

We got out of the bus and started walking through the first corridor that leads to the rotunda (the center hub of the cell blocks). We walked right by the cell Al Capone inhabited on his stay there. His room is very dressy and classy. He had it good in there.

It was mass chaos arriving into the rotunda with all 99 other guests plus celebs. There were 8 celebrities total as well. Each of them would pair up and take a group down a particular cell block. We were chosen to go down cell block 2 first. This cell block consisted of two corridors we could explore; we could also go outside and visit solitary confinement and the outside grounds. We did EVP sessions with one of the celebrities and did indeed get answers from the ghosts right then and there. I kept sneaking away from the crowd when possible to video several of the cells and try to get a reaction on my own. I did keep feeling like there were spider webs going across my face and on my arms. Later I was told that there were not any spider webs and maybe one or two other people where having the same experience out of the huge group we were with. I have heard of the "spider webbing" effect before but never actually experienced it. Supposedly it is when a spirit is touching you. I am not sure if that is a fact but it sure was strange that someone walked through a dark corridor right before me said that there were not any webs yet I walked through right after and kept feeling it across my face and arms.

We went through all the cell blocks we could and did several EVP sessions, Shack Hack sessions, Ovilus Sessions, and of course the old provoking method. I did hear footsteps at the end of one hall that had the outside door shut. There was no one down there and come to find out several other people throughout the weekend had heard the same noise when no one was down that hall.

We did an EVP session up in Cell Block 12 which is supposed to be the most active area in the place. People throughout the night had been scratched and bit. I was very excited and tried to provoke responses myself. I did not get harmed but at a couple points I did feel warm breathing on the back of my neck. I had people next to me that were witnesses that no one was behind me that we could actually see. There were several EVPs caught by many people that night. Unfortunately I did not get anything on my personal recorder. I sat in a cell all by myself and did not have anything happen. I think this was what my guide had told me about when he said if I did not focus and relax I would not hear anything from the ghosts. I was beginning to know exactly what was going on for me. I hadn't practiced what he told me after I left his office and I was now yielding the results. Shame on me for not listening to him!

Another cell block had interesting results although still not as intense as I would have liked. We were doing a "Shack Hack" session. A Shack Hack is a little FM/AM radio that has been modified to do a continuous scan through the stations. Supposedly it allows a ghost to grab onto certain words and basically answer you in real time.

We started our session and my video camera shut off. I turned it back on and ask who turned it off. The response on the shack hack was "Sam". So they were definitely there for sure. Someone had asked if they were upstairs watching us and the response was "why don't ya come up here". It was a woman's voice. We had been told that particular cell block had been for women at one time. After it started to become nearly over crowded, they removed the women from the prison and placed them elsewhere. So the fact that it was a woman's voice definitely gave credibility to that area.

I decided to pick a cell and sit in it by myself. I had my video camera running as well as my recorder and unfortunately did not get anything of interest on there. I could hear whispering but I was fairly certain it was other guests walking around exploring on their own. It was very interesting though to sit in a cell alone. I did it twice that night and learned that I could actually do it. I was not sure beforehand if I could handle something like that or not. I proved to myself that I absolutely can.

That night was a night to remember and I have a lot of video footage placed on my youtube channel that is accessed through my website.

The next day we went to more seminars and then we had an auction to which I won a private investigation with two of the celebrities along with six other people. This was a chance of a lifetime and I was not passing it up. All proceeds went to the funding of restoring Eastern State Penitentiary so it was good for everyone all the way around. It got down to me as well as four other people and we were the final winners of this particular auction. I was so excited. I was going to get to investigate yet another night at the prison with much less people so much less chance of evidence contamination.

After winning the auction I was not sure how I was going to get to the prison because this time they were not using buses for us small groups. They were transporting the second group back and forth. Our small group was to investigate at 2 a.m. after the other large group was finished. Luckily a friend had won the auction to go investigate with two of the other celebrities for that night so I got to ride with her. She actually lives about fifteen minutes away from the prison so we rode in her car.

We arrived at the prison just in time to see the large group leaving. We entered down the corridor stopping to look at Al Capone's cell. We arrived at the rotunda to meet our celebrity leaders as well as the rest of our groups. We were in two different groups so we had to divide up but we would meet in the rotunda after we were done.

The first destination for my group was to walk down cell block four which was incredibly dark. The door was closed at the end so we could not see anything at all. I relied on my video camera's IR light to guide me on my screen. It was the only way I could see. I will say that I tripped a couple of times because even with your video camera and IR light, you cannot perceive anything the way it should be. You think something is a foot away from you and in reality it is half of that and so you end up stumbling over it. This was the true meaning of lights out for investigating. One celebrity went first so he could open the door down at the end. We were to each go one by one taking our time to follow him. I was nominated to go first since I had the video camera with light. I walked as slow as I could and while I did, I kept feeling the spider web across my face and arms. I looked up and I thought I saw a web but when I got to the end of the corridor, the celebrity told me that there were no spider webs at all when he walked through. It was the same story with the people behind me who were also walking very fast. They were a little more scared than I was. They all said the same thing, that there were no webs.

So again, I had the "web" experience without a real web. It is entirely possible that after all my taunting the night before and my taunting as I walked, I believe they may have been touching me after all. I would have to go back and experience the same thing though to make sure that I wasn't experiencing a lone spider trailing across at just the right time landing his web in my face.

We regrouped after everyone was done walking the corridor. We were outside in the prison yard and it was time to go to our next area. We decided to go to "the hole" since they had heard about people experiencing it and had not gone. I had so I was on board with going back. When we were in there the first time people heard a door shut where there was no door as well as a voice or two.

Immediately when we arrive, one celebrity and I chose a cell to sit in and left the other people in the small corridor outside of the cell. The other celebrity sat down and geared his digital recorder up for an EVP session. We decided to do lights out completely so I had to shut my video camera screen so it didn't emit any extra light. Everyone shut off their flashlights. We began the EVP session. We tried a multitude of things to say to taunt the prisoners to communicate with us. After about fifteen or twenty minutes we decided to change positions. We had a couple of others get in the cell we were in and we went into the corridor. He decided to take the cell behind the other celebrity. It was oddly a room full of toilets. We made a lot of puns about it. We actually had hoped we could appeal to the funny side of the prisoners while provoking. Maybe they would enjoy our conversation and want to interject just as I had experienced so many times before with my group in the past.

After two EVP sessions we decided to move on. People mentioned hearing whispers, footsteps and again a door clinking when there was no door there. We started walking across the prison yard again to our next adventure. It turns out that we got lucky that night. We were allowed to go to the guard tower. First however, we ended up revisiting cell block twelve where all the violent and malevolent spirits had been attacking girls the night before. We went down the long corridor and up the stairs.

Once we got upstairs we decided some would go into individual cells again. One girl went into the cell where the reported attacks took place and the others spread out in other cells next to that one. I decided I would stay in the corridor this time, hoping that if I tried, that spirit would come out and do something else to me other than breathe on my neck like the night before. We started to do an EVP session and I tried my best to taunt this ghost. I called him names and told him to do something to me. I did feel warmth on the back of my neck again, almost burning. I asked one of the guys to check it out and see if they could see anything but there was nothing visible on my skin. No one got hurt in the infamous cell and to our knowledge we really didn't get anything evidence wise. Whatever was there must have gotten tired of dealing with so many people and went to hide out.

We went down the treacherous steps once again and back to the rotunda. We had to wait for the other group to leave the guard tower and go to another area for us to go in. It is a very small space and even smaller staircase. Some people split off and walked down some corridors alone and I decided to stay in the rotunda and try to see if any ghosts would communicate with me there. Unfortunately nothing happened.

Finally they radioed in and we were allowed to head up to the guard tower. These steps were just as treacherous as the ones in cell block twelve. Once we went up one flight we then had to ascend a tiny and narrow spiral staircase. When we reached the first landing my K-II meter began going nuts. It only lasted a few seconds though and I could not get it to repeat. I saw some electrical wires there plugged in so I scanned them with my meter as well as the outlet and got no results. Something made my meter blink but after going over all my evidence later on, I heard the lady that was guiding us and unlocking doors. She was talking on her walkie talkie at the time. I am willing to bet the signal made my meter go off. I could be wrong but it is more of a possibility that I am correct.

This is the type of thing I was explaining earlier about de-bunking. I wanted it to be something paranormal but when I reviewed evidence, I heard what I heard and knew that I had to throw the meter blinking out the window. It was contaminated and there was no way to prove that it had been her or if it was a ghost. I do not remember it blinking any other time when she was on the radio but then again she was mostly at a distance when she was talking except that one moment.

We got up to the top level and could see the whole prison from there. It was so neat to look at and we wondered how one guard would be able to keep an eye on everything at once. What was disappointing was that the group before us was got results and spoke with "the warden" up in the tower. I felt a bit envious because we did not get anything happen to our group at all. Aside from enjoying the view and a bunch of fresh air blowing around after hours of sweating, there was nothing paranormal going on for us. We were informed time was up so we had to head back down and back to the rotunda. Once back in the rotunda we moved on to the outdoors area to depart. I rejoined with my friend again as well as another lady who needed a ride back to the hotel. I kept hoping the whole time that I would have more evidence on my recorder or perhaps video camera that I did not catch live and in person. I did have a very good time though despite the lack of evidence I would have liked to have acquired.

Back to the hotel I went and when I walked in, some of my friends where reviewing evidence and talking in the lobby so I joined them. I think finally at around 6 a.m., I called it quits and went to my room to pack and try to get some sleep.

All in all it was a great trip and great adventure. I would definitely go back to Eastern State Penitentiary anytime. I would love to go in a small group and explore the whole place all night long instead of just a six hour attempt. I enjoyed meeting my friends and enjoyed being in a new to me city and relaxing. The celebrities were a lot of fun to hang out with and hopefully I will get to do it again someday.

And now after such a great time, it was time for me to board my plane on my journey back home. Part of me did not want to go home and part of me missed my boyfriend of course. I also missed all of our pets. There is always value in knowing where your home is and what is there waiting for your return.

Chapter VIII

Knowing

Do you know what the difference between a ghost, poltergeist, or spirit is? Are you sure what you encounter is one of the three? If not then I have some explaining to do for you. Based on my knowledge over the years and also with the help of some reputable mediums out there, I can help distinguish the difference so that you can go into investigation looking for the signs and signals to give you a heads up on which kind they may be.

First of all there are different kinds of entities you can come across. There are your standard ghosts which are the spirits that have not yet crossed over to the next realm. I use to believe that some did not know that they were dead and so they were wandering around looking for their family. Recently I found out that they do in fact always know they are dead. It may take them a little while but once they realize no one can see or hear them, they start to realize what is going on. Also they see their loved ones get old and die so it is foolish to think they do not know they are dead.

Ghosts either are not ready to move on because they feel they haven't had enough life, they want to watch over their loved ones, they want to stay with their most beloved object or person, or they do not know they have the option to leave and be with their already crossed over loved ones. They tend to make noise, haunt places/things, and like to make people scared on occasion. Some of them play practical jokes as well.

Spirits are those who have actually already crossed and come back to visit their loved ones to watch over them or try to guide them. They are knowledgeable and can travel anywhere at will. They do not haunt anyone and certainly do not try to scare people. They can also visit us in our dreams to let us know things are going to be ok, to warn us, or just to let us know they are ok and happy.

Poltergeists are noisy ghosts. They are the kind that want to scare people by moving objects, throwing things, making a lot of noise, stealing things and placing them in other places so they can watch you run around trying to find it. They are disturbed individuals or at least were when they were alive. They have no interest in moving on nor do they care that they are scaring someone or a family. These are the kind that cause the most problems. They want to see how far they can push people before they leave. Some of them are attached to certain places and perhaps do not wish to share their place.

Over the years there have been many names that people use to describe these beings. What are they anyway? I believe they are the energy source of our human shells. They are our souls. I have encountered even animal spirits. I have had spirits of cats curl up and purr on my bed. I would sit up and look around thinking one of my cats came in to find that the door was shut and no real cat was sitting there. This type of thing tells me that we as humans are not the only ones with souls.

When we die, our souls exit our bodies and then they become one of these words we've made up to describe them. No matter what we call them, they are still the same. The basics are those that I have explained.

Now demons are whole other category that I will not begin to explain. Since I do not really believe in them, it would be purely speculation on my behalf to try and describe what demons are and how they act. I do have many Demonologist friends that can give you any information you seek regarding this.

There are unfortunately many that claim there are demonic forces going on in their homes. There are a lot of paranormal groups that also claim demonic activity. Demons are very difficult to pin point and even one of my demonologist friends is able to tell you that most of those claims are false. It takes quite a bit for even him to believe there is something evil going on. He's seen a lot of cases and I trust his judgment.

Now yes, there are sometimes an evil feel in a place where a not so nice ghost may be lingering but keep in mind that they were once alive. If they were treating people badly, killing people, or hurting people in any way then most likely they will not change once they are in spirit form. These are the ones that can tend to create poltergeist activity. Those are the ones that make you feel fearful when you walk into a place. You can feel a heaviness that can either give you an instant headache, heart rate jumps fast and you feel chills arise. Hairs on your arms and neck may stand up in their presence. These are the kind you want to be very careful with. They want you to feel fear and they want you to go running away quickly. They are not friendly. These are the ones I tend to provoke but not in a home. You never want to make one of these angry if a family lives there because they will pay the price after you leave. Please use caution with what you say and do in regards to a ghost like this.

There are also sadly ghosts of children that linger. These are exactly the ones you want to try to help cross over. Who wants a child to linger in emotional pain looking for their loved ones? No one wants that. These are the kind you can try to communicate with toys, music, books, and anything children like when they are alive.

Trigger objects work well for many ghosts. What are trigger objects? Well they are objects that were either from that time period or directly belonged to that ghost itself. Sometimes music can be a good trigger as well. You can play what they might have listened to in their time. It helps them to feel comfortable and possibly able to open up to you. You can make it like a party for them.

Another ghost that is controversial are the popular shadow people. They are black shadows that somehow form a human shape or something that makes people believe it is not of this realm. Honestly I still do not know what they are after all the years I have experienced things. My first paranormal experience as you might remember was a shadow figure in the hallway. I do not know what it was or what it wanted but I do know it made me feel very intimidated. People have gotten photos of these things but no one has proven one way or the other what they are. They could be ghosts or they could be something of which we have no knowledge of that is in our realm. I am not sure I believe they are human spirits. I am not sure why they would portray themselves so dark.

We could entertain any ideas we could think of but the truth is, we just do not know at this time. It is up to us to keep on researching and looking for the answers and hopefully one day be able to say without a doubt what shadow figures really are.

In explaining the different types of ghosts I feel I should also mention the differences with hauntings. There are in fact different types of haunts. There are the kind that have intelligent ghosts and the type that have residual ghosts. Intelligent ones will have the ghosts you can actually communicate with and ask to move on. They tend to be the ones that are making contact with you or at least trying to get your attention. There are also haunting that are residual. Those are the ones where they stay with a location or object and they keep repeating a certain scene in their lives over and over. They keep doing the same things at the same time every day. I am not really sure if those are actual ghosts or the energy imprint of their former selves. It is hard to think that we can see or hear energy that has been imprinted on a place but if you think back to my experience in the old historical home in Florida, you remember my experiences were very strange and I wondered if it was just a very negative imprint on the place. That would not explain my named being called repeatedly though. I do think something was rubbed off into the home though that contributed to what is there now. It's almost as if the energy was strong enough for the ghosts to come and manifest themselves enough to reach out to me.

Ghosts feed on energy and so they will tend to go wherever they can find that energy. They feed off of people who are frightened or excited. This explains why some of them try to scare people out of their wits. It is easy access to the energy they need to survive in their world. I have read that they also like to frequent places that have a lot of people such as bars, movie theaters, restaurants, concerts and just about anywhere else where there is a mass volume of people that are full of energy whether it be happy, excited, or sad.

If you keep what I just said in mind then you would understand it makes sense for them to also haunt places like museums or places that will draw a crowd. I think the huge haunted places are that way because there are a lot of paranormal investigations going on there and a lot of the investigators are either very excited or very afraid so the ghosts get their energy fix and scare the wits out of the people that are there hence the reason we walk away with evidence of their existence.

Now there is another type of spirit activity that occurs all the time. Since ghosts have no bodies, they can travel anywhere they wish. They feed off of our energy so they will take it where they can. I have lived in so many different places and almost every single place has had some activity. Can I say that they were all haunted? No, I cannot! The reason why is that I believe they can pass through when they wish, get what they want and move on. These are the ghosts that come and go. You might get evidence of them having been around but unless you have repeatability going for you, most likely that will be the only time you hear from them.

Keeping that in mind, there are locations where you can go that will have activity one time you go and then the next may not have anything at all. It depends on what is going on with them and whether or not they want to come back. This is the reason we must be very careful about whether or not we call a place "haunted". If you have repeatability in a place or if you know that others have had a lot of activity in a place and you also experience something then you may claim it as such. There are also a lot of places that change over time. The ghosts may move on.

The hardest thing about investigating a client home is that you cannot know for sure whether or not their home is haunted. If you go in and can back up everything they claim, you come away with evidence you cannot disprove or explain, then yes, you have a haunted house. If you go in, and nothing happens at all while investigating, it may be a case of a ghost or two passing through when the client was there and so they had experiences. That does not make their home haunted. Most people want to believe their home is haunted so that they can either get rid of what scares them or so they can praise it and gain popularity with their friends or family. Experiences can be exciting but it does not mean anything other than you brushed arms with a ghost that was moving through. It happens more than people realize. Next time you go to the movies, look around and see if you can feel anything there. I almost always feel something when I go into the bathrooms and I am the only one in there. I have felt the same thing at places where I've gone to eat and stores that I shop at. The bathrooms seem to always draw them in. Maybe they followed me in or maybe they were already there waiting to pull energy off of people who are excited by the fact that they are on a date, with friends, shopping, or seeing an exciting movie. They are there so make no mistake about it.

It is time for us to lift the veil and start seeing things for what they are. Science wants physical evidence for them to find any of this real. If more of us started opening up our eyes or rather our "third" eyes, we could become so much more and could show the Scientists so much more. I believe I am going to start carrying around a pendulum with me when I go places. You never know what might happen.

By the way, pendulums are ok but they really are not too much different from dowsing rods or Ouija boards. The ghosts can tell you lies and you would know nothing about whether they are telling you the truth or not. The only thing you know for sure is that they are there. Dowsing rods are neat because they can actually point to where the spirit is in the room! I didn't bring them up in the equipment chapter as I do not really buy too much into them. You can certainly try them out if you wish. If you are highly attuned to the spirit world then you may be able to communicate with them effectively and know whether or not they are telling you the truth.

I can with complete confidence that ghosts cannot tell you the future. Look, they died and how would they know what your future holds if they do not even know what theirs holds? This is what makes Ouija boards so unreliable. You can get spirits to come through and tell you things but how will you know if you are talking to a spirit who has already crossed or a ghost that is here now? It's not easy. Ghosts will tell you anything to elicit the excitement that builds energy they need to feed off of. Keep that in mind next time you play with an Ouija board.

I hope this chapter has helped clear up some myths and helped you to form your own opinions as that is the most important thing here. Take everything I say with a grain of salt, stay skeptical and see what you see or hear on your own. It is my greatest wish that you keep this information somewhere in the back of your mind when you investigate and know all of your options. Keep everything in perspective and then do your analysis afterward and see what you come up with. Remember that ghosts are the energy of the being they use to be.

Chapter IX

Equipment

To be an effective paranormal investigator you need to see every side of the coin and know when you are going in what to expect or not to expect. You need to be sure you can cover as many angles as you can. As I have said before tangible and palpable evidence is the best kind when you are sharing and presenting with others. Personal experiences are very thrilling but you can only do so much with your word. Some people will believe you and some will not. Some will want to see what physical evidence you have to support your personal experiences. It's not that they think you are crazy it's just that most people who have not experienced anything for themselves are very leery of one's word. It's actually very understandable.

To be taken seriously you must produce anything and everything you can that points out or supports claims. Remember earlier in the book I mentioned that some people make things up for attention? This is partly the reason many are skeptical about what they hear. Rightly so! In this industry it is very difficult to just take people at their word. That having been said, you must make sure you are not at the foolish end of the spectrum.

One of the ways to gather proper evidence is by using equipment. I am sure you have seen some of the things I am about to mention on television shows about the paranormal. These are not new and are very commonly used. There have been other devices come out lately that are very interesting and I do hope to try them myself one day.

The first and very basic of the equipment is a digital camera. That's right! Most of us own a digital camera or two these days. These are great tools for documentation of an area as well as a possible photo of a spirit. Spirits are not good at showing up for photos as they fade in and out so physically, it is hard to capture them quicker than they move. Perhaps a high speed photo device could shed some light on that in the future but for now we work with what we have. Some people use fancy SLR cameras which are also very nice but to start with you can use a simple camera. Use the bigger stuff for when you become more experienced.

Take lots of photos when you go in a haunted location. Take as many as your camera will hold. It is important to be able to document certain areas so that if something comes up you can go back later and reference it easily. Always make sure to create a folder on your computer that labels where you were and what date it was. This will make it easier for you to go back to later if you need to. There isn't any advice I can really give you other than to take as many photos as possible. Look for anything strange that was not in the picture before or after. If you cannot figure it out, show it to others and get an opinion or even consult a photo expert. There are a lot of things that can be explained by camera shutter speed, lights, etc. We cannot assume right away that if we see something unusual that it is paranormal. You have to do the research. Did something happen at that particular time that you can back up with other evidence? Can you rule interference out? Are you sure someone wasn't smoking? These are things you have to ask yourself when you go back over your photos. Scour them as best you can. If you find interesting things you cannot explain, put them in another folder so that when you go back over corresponding evidence maybe you can link them together or rule them out.

Next piece of equipment that you should start out with is a digital recorder. These are very handy and can actually gather quite a bit of evidence. I prefer to use the kind that I can plug into my computer and upload all my data. It makes it very convenient for reviewing. I can turn up my speakers and hear everything. Also it lowers the risk of a tape bleeding through if you were using an analog recorder. I have actually experienced that and it was a huge disappointment. It ruined the whole investigation that had been recorded. We could not keep it because the whole thing was contaminated. Digital recorders make it so that doesn't happen. It is quite impossible.

When you start recording at a location, you must state your name, who you are with, where you are, and time. This has to be done so that if later you hear a voice, you can reference back to who was with you and know whether or not it was them or if it was a voice that shouldn't be there. If anyone coughs, whispers or shuffles, you really need to make sure and document that as well by saying "that was me" or whoever it was. Trust me when I tell you it makes all the difference in the world to know it is someone who was with you or even you yourself. Most investigations I have been on are for several hours and you will not remember every little thing about your investigation. If it is documented and you are reviewing your evidence then you hear a whisper, you know if it was someone with you or not. Sometimes jeans or pants rubbing against each other make noise and when you do a playback you hear something and figure it is a whisper. There are so many variables it is impossible to know without properly recording.

When you are walking around, try staying for several minutes in the locations that you know for sure have the most activity as per told by your group leader or by the client themselves. You want to give those areas extra attention. Ask a lot of questions that you believe they might answer. Talk to them as if they are still alive and you are trying to hold a conversation with them. Remember that most of them do not answer questions like what you see on television. Ask unique questions if you can. If they died a certain way, bring that up. If they were from a certain time period, ask them about that culture or music from that time. Anything you think would interest them to talk to you is typically the best route.

Since we are talking about questions to ask the spirits, let me just say that taunting is not always the best route. You do not want to ask a murder victim, or rather demand they appear before you. They will not take kindly to this and they will run from you or refuse to talk to you. With children, murder victims or victims of horrible tragedy, you want to be nice and ask them nice questions or if you know anything about them, make conversation.

I personally only taunt when I am in a location where there are bullies, criminals, prisoners, etc. If they are hurting people then I want to get down to the bottom of it and let them know it is not o.k. to do this to people. Those I will do whatever I can to get to repeat what they have done to others onto me. Otherwise when I'm in a place like a mental hospital, I will generally be nice and ask nice questions. I will sympathize with them.

Places that are wide open with a crazy history, I am generally pretty nice until I do not get a response. Then I will taunt mildly. Typically whoever I am with and I will hold a conversation we think might interest the spirits and they end up giving us their input in between our sentences. It's very interesting but it is effective.

When reviewing your audio you have to be very alert. It is very difficult to sit for hours and review audio. You also want to make sure you have the proper software so that you are able to grab a clip and make it into format to share. I personally use Audacity. It's free and it works very well. Also you want to make sure to have noise eliminating earphones or a quiet house in which to work. Sometimes you can easily miss a voice if you aren't able to hear fully. It is very time consuming but worth it when you find something you can rule out as being anyone who was with you. It's an amazing feeling to capture your first EVP. It gives you a sense of satisfaction knowing you finally got something to prove that something other than the living was talking. I remember the first one I had gotten. It was very exciting and it made me want to do it more and more.

Just like you catalog the photos, make sure you catalog your audio. You'll want to make a new folder to put all of your "could be" EVP's into a folder of their own so later you can upload them to the internet if you wish. It's much easier to share with people if you upload to the internet. That is just something for you to keep in mind if you are planning on becoming an investigator.

Next piece of equipment I'd like to tell you about is the K-II meter. This meter is fantastic for picking up on abnormal amounts of Electromagnetic Fields. Unlike it's the EMF detector that everyone knows and still sometimes uses, it is less jumpy. In other words, it will pick up the stronger EMF rather than all EMF. You can walk up to an outlet and unless it's turned on, it will not pick it up. So if all the lights are out and nothing is plugged in at a location, it is most likely not going to make your meter do anything. You do still have to treat it as an EMF detector however. Keep in mind that when you are using this device, you need to walk around the whole room and try to pick up on anything. The reason is so that if something does cause the meter to go off and you know it was nothing electrical, then you may have something.

I will tell you that when it lights up totally solid and stays that way, it is some kind of interference that is not paranormal. Paranormal disturbances will cause the meter to flash in no uncertain pattern. Now if it does flash, start asking them questions and get them to do it a few more times. If it does, it is something intelligent and you want to be sure to back it up with your group or whoever you are with. You can use this to get them to answer yes or no questions. You can tell them to make it flash once for yes or two for no. However you want to get them to communicate this is a pretty neat tool to use. I would make sure someone with a video camera is nearby to document what is going on. That gives you tangibility.

EMF meters. I do not currently posses one of these as I use my K-II mainly. EMF meters can give you a good base reading around the room at where the levels should be so if it spikes suddenly in an area where it wasn't before, you may have something. I would highly recommend if you use one, please make sure you get one that doesn't make noise. I use to own one that was very noisy which is not good for your recorders or video cameras. It can also contaminate someone else's evidence if they are in another room and their recorders pick up on it.

Now what I am about to tell you is pure speculation of some. Some groups believe that high EMF levels in an area can cause people to hallucinate, get dizzy, hear things, and see things. With my boyfriend being an Electrical Engineer, I can honestly tell you that he says that it does not do those things. He builds and plays with Tesla Coils professionally and recreationally. He has been playing with electricity for years and some of his best friends are in the same industry and can tell you. So before you tell a client or anyone else that an area is causing them to believe they hear, see something, or feel uncomfortable in a certain area is simply due to high EMF, please think again. There is nothing on the internet that is a scientific fact. If you look, there are studies but none of them have been validated and even Wikipedia says that there is not enough scientific evidence to prove it either way. There are only small test that have been done. Until we can have science teams sit down and test hundreds or even thousands of people under certain conditions with high EMF then you cannot assume that is what is going on. Now I will say that if you do find high EMF, please alert the client as they could have bad wiring that needs to be repaired so it does not cause a short out or fire in their home. Sending a client on their way letting them believe their experiences were not paranormal can be damaging later on.

Tell them what they need to know and continue your investigations. I would still try to do an evp session as well as a video camera in that area. You may get something that has nothing to do with EMF arise. Also you would be either debunking that area or giving credibility which is what the client is after. If at all possible, if they had high EMF and you had them get it repaired, go back later and investigate again.

I know I said be skeptical when you go into an investigation but you also need to be open to possibilities at the same time. The EMF issue is one of those that does deserve attention and maybe multiple investigations to get to the root of the issue. You may find that there was something there after all and the client was not just physically affected by an electrical source.

So far we have covered digital cameras, digital voice recorders and EMF detectors. Next I would like to tell you about video cameras. I use a video camera that has night shot as I mentioned in an earlier chapter. This provides some light you cannot see unless you are looking through the display screen. This is an infrared light that makes it possible to see in the dark. Having an extra one or two of these is also a good idea if you can afford it. It will give you more visibility range and will help you avoid running into something and hurting yourself. There is always the chance of that happening in low light because again, all you can see is on the screen and that throws your perception of what is actually in front of you. It's kind of like a rear view mirror on a car. It seems they are close but when you turn around and look, they are actually close than what it looks like in your mirror. It is exactly the same way when you are viewing through the video camera. So be very careful when you are walking around. It can be very dangerous.

You will need extra batteries if you are doing a long investigation. You want to make sure your video camera can stay up and going the whole time so you don't miss anything. Now if you are using stationary cameras set up in certain rooms then it is ok as long as you can plug them into an outlet that is active. Most houses and businesses will have them. It is a little tricky in locations where there is no electricity at all. In those cases you should have a lot of backup or some kind of charged up battery source that you can plug into to recharge. Some groups carry car chargers that they can simply go recharge real quick in their vehicle. There are also huge car battery size chargers that you can fill up and then carry it into the building with you to your central location so that when it becomes necessary you can go recharge and get right back to what you were doing.

My video camera has a thirty gig hard drive. I thought that should be plenty but I must say, an all night event takes up a huge portion of that hard drive so if you get the kind I have, it also has a slot for extra SD Memory. It comes in handy when you have long nights. You will need extra space on your computer as well if you are going on several investigations. You can use an external hard drive to stick all of your investigation stuff on.

You also always want to have an Infrared Non-Contact Thermomcter as well. The meter is a point and shoot thermometer that you see the television groups using. This will help you determine quick temperature changes. Also I have used it as a device to communicate before. I have gotten them to drop the temperature of my choice a few times. This little device comes in very handy.

When you go to use this, you must get a base reading around the room. What temperature is the average in the room? Note that windows and floors will be a different temperature as will the ceilings and floors. Heat rises so it will be slightly warmer up higher than it will be below. Just take notes on a notepad on what temperatures were in a particular room. If you get a drastic change all the sudden, start asking questions just like you would with anything else. See if you can get them to manipulate the thermometer again. See if you can follow the abrupt coldness or abrupt heat. Are there windows open? Is there air conditioning or central heat? You have to investigate every angle before you can assume it is paranormal.

The tools I have listed for you are a very basic list of tools I currently own and use for myself. They are very good to start with for a beginner. Even if you only have one or two of these things to start with, you will be in good shape. It takes a lot of practice to do this right. Most of us that have been doing it for years still can get rusty. I know if I haven't been on a trip in months, I have to go somewhere and do a practice run again to make sure I can remember everything I need to.

You'll want to start out with simple places. Go to places that are outdoors or go on one of the big events that many of the famous groups offer. You are along with a huge number of people trying to learn the same thing. The people running it will do their best to teach you their methods.

What I have explained to you is just my method for doing things. My methods work for me but may not work for you. You have to do this several times before you actually start to develop your own style and can figure out what is effective for you and your group. The best way to learn by far is to get out there and practice as often as you can.

I do recommend you do not start doing home investigations for clients until you have a comfortable level of experience first. As I mentioned go to well known places and investigate those first. Get plenty of evidence review experience as well as on location experience.

Take your time organizing your group if that is what you plan on doing. You will need to choose members who reflect what you are looking for. You need to be sure they are dependable and can fit well with your own personality. It is not easy to put together the right people but it is possible and does get done. The best way to do this is to establish what your goals are and what you would expect from a group. The next thing is to interview people who are interested in joining. Come up with your own list of questions that you think would be important for them joining the group.

Once you have your group and you will need to train them with the experience you now have. Make sure they understand your equipment, how to use it and how to conduct an investigation. I even went through a legal perspective with mine. I wrote up waivers for all my members to sign so that if they get hurt on the job, they knew it was their responsibility to seek medical attention. It's not saying you don't trust your members, it is so that they know that if they do not listen to what you have told them to stay safe, and they have to now care for themselves. It's a very good thing to have on hand. You also want waivers for guests so that they know the same deal. I do not recommend anyone under 18 going unless they have a parent or guardian with them. In the event you know a young person who is very mature for their age, you can make an exception but a parental form should also be drawn up so that the parent can sign that as well as the waiver making them responsible for their child. You always want to have every angle covered.

When you begin doing home investigations there are a few forms that must also be drawn up and signed as well. You have to have a consent form from the client thus giving you permission to enter and investigate their home. You will also need to sit and write several questions that you will want to ask the client so you are fully armed when you are live. You want to ask obvious questions such as which rooms are the most active, what happened there, who did it happen to, has it happened again, and other questions similar to this.

All you want to tell the client is that you will do your best to see what you can find and you will share with them later if you did find anything. Do not scare the client. I found it was always better to have them go somewhere for a few hours to allow us to investigate their home without them being there. If you get something and someone on your team gets excited, it could potentially scare the client or get them excited when it may have been nothing at all. It's just more professional to wait until after all evidence has been reviewed to tell the client anything at all. You need to have your documented proof to present to the client on a different day. You can share your personal experiences with them as well but unless you have a lot of tangible evidence to support it, you are really giving the client false hope. And again, this is my opinion and I try to see how a client would see things. You always need to look at both sides of a coin. Do you want to mis-inform them so they can go tell their friends and family that their house is haunted when really it was just Grandma Jo checking up on them periodically from the other side? No of course not. That is bad data. Our job is to give them truth. If we have a lot of evidence supporting a haunting then by all means, share that information so they can decide how they want to proceed. If they are afraid but evidence points to something very mellow and maybe a little playful, let them know it is ok and they can ask the spirit to move on or stop scaring them. It gives the client their power back.

When you receive a phone call from a worried parent that says something is scaring their children then by all means get out there as quick as you can. No one wants children to be tormented needlessly. As I mentioned before, be very careful what you tell them, investigate everything thoroughly and then share your data with them if you are sure it was nothing that could be explained. Be as honest as you can but reveal the data in a very cool, calm way. You do not want to upset them in any way. If it something you feel is out of your realm then make sure you contact another group or person who has experience and can help them. Always do what you can to help the client. If that means calling someone else, please do not be prideful and neglect calling someone for reinforcement.

Investigating clients homes are much more extensive and can be stressful. You have so many rules you must follow. So if you are starting a group, please keep these things in mind and it should help you determine whether you will be the type of group that investigates well known places only or if you only do client homes. In some cases, you might feel compelled to do both. Whatever you feel you can handle then that is the route you should go. Just please consult with other people and/or groups that can give you their insight. We are all out there and we are all here to help people.

So now that you have been armed with a bunch of information, I do hope you make a wise choice. Know that there are plenty of us investigators out in the field that are more than happy to answer your questions in helping you get started. I recommend networking as much as you can. Get online and find as many people in the industry as you can. Try to setup investigations with some of them if it is at all possible.

Invest in equipment you planning on using for a long time. I know that something I still very much wish to obtain is a Thermal Imaging Camera. These are cameras that pick up on heat or cold signatures and in some cases pick up on apparitions walking in front of the camera. Those are very high quality cameras and can cost a lot. That would not be a first piece of equipment you would want to buy obviously unless someone offers you a great deal that you cannot pass up. I sure wish that would come my way. Maybe it will sometime when I least expect it.

Lastly respect each other in the field. We all do things differently and just because you have your method, does not make someone else's wrong. Remember none of us are experts. If we were there would be real schools and degrees for this but to date, there are none. There are some fake sites out there that certify you but I can assure you, they will certify anyone. There is no such thing as a Certified Paranormal Investigator. Keep yourself level, informed, and respect other groups or individuals you come across.

In this industry there are a great many people or groups that do not have that respect for others and unfortunately it always ends up bad. Names end up getting trashed all over the internet and some end up disbanding because someone has trashed their name so bad that no clients will touch them. It's sad but it does exist so just try to remember that most of us are all out for the same thing which is to discover what is out there and help people to the best of our ability. If we can also help a few ghosts cross over then so be it. The more the merrier is what I say. Always come out with the better equipment, better connections, better EVP's, better this or that. Again, do not get cocky like that or you will have that chance of being black barred by the community and that is not something you want to have happen.

I am in this industry because it is my life's passion. Ever since I was a child, I have wanted nothing more than to produce evidence that there are in fact, ghosts in this world. I will probably do this until I am old and have one foot in the grave. I live for it. Some paranormal investigators go even further and delve into UFO's, Bigfoot, Etc, but Ghosts has always been my niche. So here I am folks. I am here right now sharing all my life and information with you and I hope it has helped you get a good idea of whether you want to start doing this yourself. I encourage you to do more homework after you are done reading my book. There is vast knowledge out there to be had and it's just waiting for us to take the plunge.

If after reading this you still want to remain just an enthusiast, there is nothing wrong with that either. Now you have knowledge of what investigators know and so when you watch television shows you will be able to see and know different angles that maybe you didn't know before. You are now armed with data which was my goal all along with this book.

I do not know how many of you will now go out there and start your own group and will possibly seek my advice further but I am here for you. I implore you to visit my website or email me with your questions. I will try to help you to the best of my ability and if I cannot I certainly have many friends that can and will help. Thank you so much for taking the time to read my book. I do hope that at a very minimum you were entertained and at the maximum you were inspired to start investigating for yourself. Good luck out there and I do wish you well friends!

As for me, I have many more adventures to come and much more data to share with you but that will be for another book. In the meantime I will be sharing and posting all of the data I get onto my website. Bless you all

To write me with any questions you may have, please see my website:

http://www.jendevillier.com

Printed in Great Britain
by Amazon.co.uk, Ltd.,
Marston Gate.